This book is dedicated to my mother and sister; to my late father, who brought me to play; and to my late grandfather, who taught me to play.

This book is also dedicated to you, who seeks to improve every day in every way . . . especially when it involves ball striking and touch around the greens.

PRAISE FOR
Let Go, Let Golf

"A cross between Harvey Penick's *Little Red Book* and Marcus Aurelius' *Meditations* (with a touch of Eugen Herrigel's *Zen in the Art of Archery*), John Rota's *Let Go, Let Golf* turns this crazy game into a portal to mindfulness and pure, egoless aspiration. By the end of chapter 1, I felt a sense of calm and composure. Halfway through, I could begin to feel the flow. By the time I finished, I felt like I had a mindset and a grounding in internal reality that would serve me not just on the golf course but in every aspect of life. Bravo, Mr. Rota. And the illustrations by Vic Juhasz are great!"

STEVEN PRESSFIELD, bestselling author of *The Legend of Bagger Vance*

"If you're looking for a better way to up your game, *Let Go, Let Golf* is the book for you. Brimming with witty quips, sage advice, and wisdom applicable to any sport, John Rota seamlessly guides you to a perfect score."

MERRIL HOGE, inspirational speaker, former ESPN analyst and NFL running back

"Mindset is everything in competitive sports. Mastering the art of letting go is the key to unlocking your peak performance in golf. John Rota's *Let Go, Let Golf* offers profound and often humorous advice, presenting a contemplative perspective on the intertwining aspects of life, sports, and personal growth."

LOFA TATUPU, former NFL All-Pro linebacker

"In the high-pressure world of running a business, maintaining a winning mindset is just as crucial as having a solid strategy. John Rota's *Let Go, Let Golf* is not just a book about golf; it's a guide to developing the mental fortitude needed to succeed in any competitive endeavor."

DIANE ELLIS, advisor, board director, and former retail CEO

"While I am admittedly not a golfer (which would be obvious if you saw me take a swing), this fantastic book is filled with powerful, relevant lessons. The principles in *Let Go, Let Golf*–on concepts like mindfulness, resilience, and purposeful practice–have such high utility and can be applied to every area of life and business!"

ALAN STEIN, JR., keynote speaker and author of *Raise Your Game*

"*Let Go, Let Golf* is an inspirational read. It is so good that as a non-golfer, I wanted to pick up some clubs. The endless lessons laid out will not only help you improve your game but, more importantly, enhance the quality of your life. This is a must-read."

DES HAGUE, bestselling author, nine-time CEO, and cofounder of Nebula9 Spirits

"*Let Go, Let Golf* is so much more than an instruction manual—it's a gateway to a new approach to golf and life. I was pleasantly surprised by the depth of wisdom John Rota shares that goes beyond just improving your handicap. The connections he makes to Stoic philosophy and the importance of being present were totally unexpected in a golf book but offer powerful tools for the mental game. John's insights on dealing with negativity bias, getting out of your comfort zone, and harnessing the power of momentum don't just apply on the course but in meeting any challenge. *Let Go, Let Golf* shows how the trials and triumphs of golf can teach us about ourselves and enrich our lives off the links too. It's a fun and enlightening read for anyone, whether you're a scratch golfer or just an occasional duffer (like me)."

FRANKIE RUSSO, eight-time Inc. 500 entrepreneur and bestselling author of *Breaking WHY*

"My dad taught me how to play golf when I was very young, and we had some of our best bonding moments on the course. *Let Go, Let Golf* enabled me to reflect back on all the wonderful experiences with my dad together on a golf course. I was taught numerous life lessons while playing golf with my best friend, and this book allowed me to recall all of them! Thank you, John Rota, for a wonderful read."

MATT GUTERMUTH, CEO of iControl Data Solutions and amateur golfer

"The mental game makes or breaks champions. In golf, letting go of tension is a better decision faster and the secret to unlocking your best swing. *Let Go, Let Golf* by John Rota provides insightful and lighthearted guidance. You'll learn how to relax, focus, and find your optimal performance on the course. It's the best decision you can make."

PAUL EPSTEIN, former NFL and NBA executive; bestselling author of *Better Decisions Faster* and *The Power of Playing Offense*

"As a seasoned executive and former member of Team USA, I highly recommend *Let Go, Let Golf* for its transformative insights and practical approach in both business and life. Inspired by golf greats, it combines intentional living with structured training, providing valuable techniques and drills for players seeking to elevate their skills."

KEITH KING, former international president, chief legal and talent officer at Centerplate

"This book isn't just for golfers! It teaches anyone to slow down, trust their instincts, and find success in all aspects of life. By quieting the mind and visualizing goals, you can unlock your true potential on and off the course."

PAT MAHAN, host of the *Like Attracts Like* podcast

amplify
an imprint of Amplify Publishing Group

www.amplifypublishinggroup.com

Let Go, Let Golf: Mindful Ways to Practice with Purpose

Illustrations by Victor Juhasz
https://juhaszillustration.com/

For more information, please contact:
Amplify Publishing, an imprint of Amplify Publishing Group
620 Herndon Parkway, Suite 220
Herndon, VA 20170
info@amplifypublishing.com

Library of Congress Control Number: 2024904659
CPSIA Code: PRV0524A
ISBN-13: 979-8-89138-065-3

Printed in the United States

Let Go, Let Golf

Mindful Ways to Practice with Purpose

JOHN ROTA

Illustrations by Victor Juhasz

amplify

an imprint of Amplify Publishing Group

CONTENTS

UROBOROS

It's new all the time.

Like the eternal cycle of the uroboros, improving your game is a never-ending project.

To get better at golf (or anything, for that matter) you have to give it your full attention. The goal of this book is to help you to get to that place of intentional living to connect your mind, body, and soul to your capabilities—that beautiful balance between enjoyment and focused attention. Playing well is a blissful journey with a love of practice and an appreciation for the process. This is the basis of personal transformation and a much better golf game.

Practicing with purpose is the ultimate way to hone your craft. Training with structure simplifies the game of golf and helps you get the most out of the time you *do* have to hit the range.

Train like you do muscle groups: get your reps in and focus on specific aspects of your game. You are not there to be a generalist and bang out a mindless bucket. You are there to mindfully improve.

Your intention is to play good golf.

This book is your mental time in the dirt.

These stories are for low and high handicappers alike who are looking to reach the next plateau. The mindful stories, drills, and games are for any level player who wants to improve while they compete with themselves. They will help you un-think, turn your analytical brain off, and forget about everything but your present shot.

The idea for *Let Go, Let Golf* is inspired by classic golf books. It's a small nod to legends like Harvey Penick and Ben Hogan, whose unique points of view and timeless knowledge are an eternal beacon of light to all golfers. Hogan's *Five Lessons* and Penick's *Little Red Book* are arguably the most important instructional golf books ever written. The simple eloquence of how they decode the game is as practical as it is soulful.

This book is your mental time in the dirt.

This grinder's handbook is a collection of philosophical thoughts from an amateur's point of view that offers effective, down-to-earth ideas on how to develop your golf swing, as well as entertaining ways for how you can approach the mental game.

Some of the things you will learn are:

- How to get into your zone quicker—it's easier than you think.
- A new way to keep score—forget about the number on your card.
- How to effectively practice at home—it will boost your confidence.
- An efficient way to aim your ball—it's right in front of you.

This handbook also includes fun mental *and* physical drills any player can do on the course, practice range, or at home to improve skills and sharpen competitive spirit. The stories are intended to raise your emotional set point and your vibration as a player.

Don't just read this book—*practice* it. Let this volume serve as a contemporary way to help you become a better player. Perhaps it can also serve as a rite of passage to the genre of golf books that inspired it. My wish is that you go down that rabbit hole: practice with purpose and joyfully improve your game.

—John Rota

— ONE —
LET GO

MINDFUL BUCKET

TO CHANGE YOUR LIFE, you have to change the way you think. To improve your golf game, you have to change the way you think about practicing.

Playing games while you practice is a way to optimize your time in the dirt. It keeps your mind engaged with each shot and ultimately helps you improve much faster than you normally would just banging out a mindless bucket at the range on the few occasions you get to go.

Be present at the range by making keen observations of your surroundings. Notice the difference in how the better players hit balls. The seasoned players are hitting more wedges and short irons, picking out targets, and making sure they are getting feedback with each shot. They are (more than likely) hitting off the grass and will work through a progression of short irons first, then mid-irons, long irons, and finishing with their woods.

It is highly recommended to hit off the grass. A mat will not give you accurate feedback and can also be harsh on your wrists and elbows. When you see a seasoned player hitting off the grass, they will often leave what I refer to as a *pro-style patch*—a singular divot patch or efficient line that rips up as little turf as possible. They do not leave the range with potholes all over their hitting area. Don't be that guy.

Your mind and attitude are the key indicators of how well you'll perform.

Imagine each ball you hit costs one hundred dollars. That changes your thinking, doesn't it? Being mindful means you pick a target for each and every shot. It also keeps your attention engaged by playing different games to challenge yourself, helping you remain keenly focused. You can work on shaping your ball a specific, deliberate way, you can grip up on the club and hit low stingers to simulate playing on a windy day, and you can even take aim at the ball guy. Do not waste a swing.

You can perfect your pre-shot routine by imagining what you would like to do with each ball, then execute. Like anything involving visualization, you will be astonished at how well you hit when you imagine the shot first. If your ball is not going exactly how you envision, that is okay—welcome to golf. Work through it until your thoughts match your physical reality. The goal of hitting a mindful bucket is to improve your mental and physical game simultaneously.

Your mind and attitude are the key indicators of how well you'll perform. It's all in your head. How and what you think can allow your greatness to come out.

BUDDHA GOT GAME

Mindfulness is the energy of focused attention. It is the practice of being fully alive in each moment, finding the space inside yourself to be completely present to what is happening within and around you. In both life and golf, the benefit of practicing mindfulness is the awareness that peace and joy are readily available to you in every moment. The formula is simple: whatever you do, do with your whole being.

We tend to avoid the here and now, living in a seemingly infinite pattern of habitual energy, a loop running much of our lives. We are almost always multitasking. We are addicted to scrolling through our phones, checking emails, texting, watching social media, reading endless news headlines…the list goes on. It is the mundane, everyday circle we frequently live in with our routines and unconscious daily rituals that can set us back. Use golf and time in nature to break the loop.

The more we can utilize mindfulness to be aware and break the cycle of habitual energy, the more we can remind ourselves that we are free to live fully in the now.

Why not focus on your golf game?

Being in the now is what it takes to improve and genuinely enjoy the game.

Mindfulness can happen in a single breath or a single footstep. As you become accustomed to this practice, it can lead to a new form of relaxation. This will no doubt result in an improvement in the quality of your life.

Like your golf skills, mindfulness gets easier with training. We can intellectually understand this way of life, but it still takes practice to master in action. Allowing mindfulness to be second nature will transform how you take on challenges or deal with pain. It is our Buddha nature. We have direct access to this every day: the power to gain enlightenment, to create our best life.

Access your power by playing golf. Use the time practicing and playing as a meditation with mindfulness—awareness that helps you focus and stay present. It quiets your mind and nervous system, allowing good thoughts to flow.

IT WORKS IN REVERSE

Just go hit balls.

Without getting overly technical or mechanical, just swing your swing. No overthinking. Aim and hit the golf ball where you intend.

Easier said than done? Yes.

When it comes to learning your golf swing, there is no magic recipe. You have to go find it in the dirt. You have to hit balls.

Learn your swing through repetition. Feel the nuances of various shots. Watch players like yourself—or better—at the range. Examine their moves on the ball. Yes, take a lesson and watch online videos, read articles and books. The bottom line is: you *have* to hit balls. The only place you will find your tempo and consistent good-shot feeling is digging it out in the dirt.

Practicing with a club in your hands, getting your grip right, visualizing, then executing a golf shot—it's all about *feel* as you're contorting your arms into the right angles, your hands in the right position, your hips turning through the swing, to get the ball flying where you are aiming. It may not be pretty (yet), but you're golfing your ball. The technical talk will make more sense *after* you learn how to hit a good ball.

You have to work with your hands to get the feel. Work on chipping and putting. Chipping is a benchmark for the whole swing. It's all in your hands: the feel of the impact zone as the blade hits the ball. With a chip, you can practice every shot in the book because you're feeling the ball impact with the clubface, computing the trajectory, and familiarizing yourself with the bounce of the blade. Next time you're on the range, it's a highly effective drill to chip with every club in the bag and feel the impact zone with all degrees—hit with all clubs to the 100-yard flag.

Learn the grip first. The grip is your one point of contact with the club. Any deficiencies in the grip will likely manifest themselves in swing flaws. In his book *Five Lessons*, Ben Hogan said, "When a golfer has completed his left-hand grip, the V formed by the thumb and forefinger should point to his right eye."[1]

Grip your club at home and take practice swings. Get used to the feeling of a golf club in your hands and the proper interlock or overlap. Be comfortable in your position over the ball.

Optimize your time at the range—and at home—by being efficient and focused while you build a bedrock of golf skills. Here are four helpful points to give you a solid practice foundation:

1. ***Get a grip.*** Understand the simple mechanics of a golf grip and how the club head is a direct extension of your hands.

2. ***Aim and fire.*** Pick your spot. What is the yardage? What club do you hit that far? Go with it and commit.

3. ***Swing your swing.*** Do what you do consistently, and you will start seeing consistency. Figure it out for yourself.

4. ***Pay attention.*** Have awareness of your tendencies. Watch every shot with every club, note where the golf ball lands, and how it feels off the clubface.

Use the data to inform you of what to practice. Go with what you got and do what you do—but go deeper. Be self-aware of *what* you are doing, *when* you are doing it, *how* and *why*. Study yourself, make proper adjustments, and find your consistent swing within all of that.

There is no question that you should analyze the golf swing, but don't let the analysis weigh you down with too much jargon, buzzwords, and clichés. Just go to a driving range and hit every club in your bag. You don't want to just pound ball after ball and engrain bad habits. Be aware and hit each ball with a purpose. Wield your sword for battle, know you're there to train your game, and commit to the work it takes to improve.

It works in reverse—get the ball going where *you* want it to go, and you'll realize that you actually have a golf swing. Develop your vanilla stock shot—your go-to when there's pressure. When you play, commit to a shot shape and aim for the middle of the green. Play for bogey when compromised. Stay away from making sixes.

Work on your lag putting. Focus on the last three to five feet. Every putt is makeable. Pick a spot and just hit a good putt. They will start to fall.

If you are serious about getting better, then *hit*, *chip*, and *putt*. Take your mind off all the advice and just swing freely. Don't be afraid of embarrassment on the range. We've all been there!

SWINGING MEDITATION

The awareness that mindfulness is accessible to you is half the battle. Make the effort to be intentional when you practice and play golf, especially when you walk around the course.

Walking meditations give you space inside yourself. They open up a channel within you where you can simply observe and look at your life, your goals, and your state of mind from a 10,000-foot view. If you practice walking meditations along the golf course, it makes for a much more rewarding experience.

Note the number of steps you take as you breathe in and out. You can practice walking meditation by counting your steps. When you walk, there is no need to rush—unless you play slow and the group behind you is asking to play through. As your lungs fill with oxygen, remain conscious of each step. Then be aware of how many steps you take as your lungs empty. Count both your breath and your steps.

The power of pause during a round—or even just a few minutes per day—is also an invitation for grace, introspection, and creativity. Take time to imagine your next shot, to check in with your body, to hydrate or nourish yourself. It is all too easy to get hung up on stress, anger, and disappointment. Instead, chill out, smile, and breathe. Your grin will create a sense of joy and calm, which helps keep you focused.

While you're out in nature, take note of all the beautiful living things that surround you in the moment. Allow gratitude and happiness to fill your soul. No matter what is going on in your world, use this time to be your best self. If we focus solely on the destination, we lose the fun and adventure of the journey itself.

Don't waste your time fretting about how you're playing or what your opponent is doing. Stay within yourself and gain perspective. Think about it: you usually don't have the time to practice, so when you *do* have that moment to yourself—man, what a cherished time to just be present and enjoy each ball you hit!

The mind is a powerful instrument. It can spin out of control with fear and anger, or it can destroy your entire practice session or round. But if we walk on the earth with a sense of love and appreciation, we can generate the energy of mindfulness, creating peace and compassion in our body, mind, and soul. This is where transformation occurs. This is happiness in a bottle. This is the way to sustained improvement and better scoring.

Incorporate these basic practices into your golf game. You will come to know the balance of breathing and walking, pausing and imagining, smiling and swinging, enjoying and being. You will come to know that golf is not just a game—it's a way of life. With each breath, each step, and each swing, we fully arrive in the present moment.

EDIE AND FERNANDO'S POOL

The lush backyard was finely manicured with blue spruces, blooming flowers, and the scent of freshly cut grass. An array of pine trees lined the property—pitch pine, pond pines, red pines—all along the fence, going downhill, bordering the neighbor's yard. An endless barrage of automobiles driving on the Garden State Parkway echoed in the distance.

The scenes of a New Jersey summer at 3 Rota Drive always included my grandfather hitting a bucket of balls against his fifteen-foot net in the yard, set up in front of the red shed where he stored his tractor and tools. As a kid, I used to always grab a club and hit dozens of balls into the net. What eleven-year-old wouldn't bang a few balls when the adults are in the house talking BS while sipping coffee?

Next door at 1 Rota Drive lived Fernando and Edie, a lovely

couple who were friends with my grandparents for years. They had a beautiful in-ground pool surrounded by flagstone in a jungle-like setting where we used to swim quite often. Their place was a full wedge away, about 111 yards downhill from the practice net.

Hitting into the net got monotonous, and out of boredom, curiosity, and a small need to find a bit of trouble, I would aim toward the pool, check if any adults were watching, and fire pitching wedges over the line of richly-colored pines. It made sense to me. I wanted to see my ball in the air and know how far it actually traveled.

The pool was my "green." It was a blind shot, so I relied on the sound of the ball landing to know where I ended up. I'd swing and wait five seconds for the *bloop* of the ball hitting water. If I heard it, I knew it was on the green in regulation (GIR). If I missed, I heard clicks off the stone, bangs off the side of the house, followed by throwing my club and sprinting to safety. Don't worry, no one was ever injured or killed.

Days later, Fernando would come over and tell my grandfather that his grandson was hitting balls again, then hand him the dozen he found in and around his pool. Fernando never seemed that angry. My grandfather would tell me not to do it again, then wink. That subtle green light let me know he trusted me—a great confidence boost for an adolescent.

I continued to hit balls in Edie and Fernando's pool whenever I visited my grandparents. It certainly helped my ball striking. The repetition created a rhythm in my swing, consistent one hundred-yard shots, over the tallest spruce, waiting for the splash.

The more I played, the more *bloops* I'd hear. I had the shot down.

Most importantly though, swinging the club outside in nature with an element of danger and challenge, marked the beginning of my love for the game of golf. It helped me see how getting better can be an enjoyable process. Practicing is often more fun than playing.

GO WITH WHAT YA GOT

The funny thing about golf is how on any given day, your swing can be *slightly* different, you can have a totally altered ball flight, trajectory, or feel than what you are accustomed to. It is not what you expect and *many times* it's unlike the day before. It can be frustrating and downright scary.

It is what it is.

This is a lesson in acceptance and adapting to *what is.* Time to improvise and own your swing of today. It could fly low or high, it can be a hook or a slap-dick willy slice. You simply do not know until you hit a ball. Adapt and adjust your game to how you are hitting at the time. Compensate and aim where appropriate. Your regular ball flight may come back during the round, perhaps your swing starts feeling more fluid, but you gotta go with what ya got while you work out the kinks.

One way to get a grip on your game and manage the stress is to do a simple breathing technique. Returning to your breath is returning to the essence of yourself. When it's hard to find your swing, the best thing to do is find yourself first. Recenter, improve your concentration and, of course, find your tempo.

Box breathing is also known as four-square breathing and involves four steps that are easily visualized in the illustration to the right. Make sure that you are breathing deeply, allowing your stomach to rise. Being aware of your breath is crucial to attaining your inner calm.

- **Step 1:** Breathe in slowly while you count to four. Feel the oxygen enter your lungs. Take notice of the rise in your chest and stomach.
- **Step 2:** Hold your breath, keeping your lungs full of air for four seconds.
- **Step 3:** Slowly exhale through your mouth, keeping your lungs empty for four seconds.
- **Step 4:** Repeat Steps 1 through 3 until you feel more relaxed.

While you are on the course, you can find a minute or two to practice box breathing and experience the immediate benefits of a calm body and a serene mind. If you have the time, maybe while you wait to tee off or you're grabbing lunch at the turn, you can practice for several minutes and experience longer-term benefits akin to meditation. The longer effects allow you to have a bit more resilience to stress and help increase the positive flow in your mind.

Remembering to breathe is the simplest way to bring you back to the here and now. It is so easy to forget when you're

1 2 3 4
HOLD YOUR BREATH
BREATHE OUT
1 2 3 4
HOLD YOUR BREATH
1 2 3 4
BREATHE IN
1 2 3 4

struggling and stressed, when your shots are flying all over the fairway and you feel like you are spending more time looking for your ball than hitting it toward a flag. We've all felt that anxiety and embarrassment. We tell ourselves, "I am so much better than this!" All the more reason why this technique is so important. When you slowly inhale oxygen, it helps you to recall that you are out on a beautiful green field playing a game you love.

Breathe your way through it. Go with what ya got. You have no choice but to work with what you have on the day.

— TWO —

IMPROVE YOUR GROOVE

THE FIVE-HOUR FRIENDSHIP

LET'S SAY YOU SHOW UP TO THE COURSE and the kid at the pro shop says you'll be paired with a random twosome or single. You grab your cart, hit a few chips and putts on the practice green, roll up to the first tee, shake hands, exchange names with a couple of new dudes in their golf shirts, and off you go—aboard the magical mystery tour that is your golf round.

The start of a new friendship begins like any other relationship, with an unofficial "getting-to-know-you" phase. While playing golf, the getting-to-know-you phase is based on two components:

1. Do you have game?
2. Are you cool?

It is always a lot more fun when the answer is yes to both.

"Do you have game?" speaks for itself. Can the person you're paired with hit the ball solidly? Or will they constantly need help looking for their ball? Do they play fast? Do they play fair? Will they keep an eye on your shots and help you locate them if needed? All of these traits play a huge role in how your round is going to go—and possibly *how you play*.

"Are you cool?" is also self-explanatory. But first, take a moment to ask yourself, "Am *I* a cool golf partner?" Will you bring your partner's putter to the green when they need it, or ask if they've got the right club? Will you share your sandwich or snacks—without being asked? The other intangibles that make one cool are also at play. Life experience, flowing conversation and jokes, astute comments after shots, and funny quips. If someone has stories to tell and a good sense of humor, these qualities are always a welcome addition to any golfing experience.

A golf round is a microcosm of life itself. The relationships we build walking the course are for a reason, season, and sometimes a lifetime. The social aspect of golf is a unique exploratory experience, like an intense five-hour crash course into the life of a stranger. You never know when you shake hands with some random player on hole number one if they will end up being in your life.

There aren't too many other sports where you spend five-plus hours with someone, conversing, swinging, competing. You can get to know a soul during that time in a unique way, not only through conversation but by the golf swing itself. Your golf swing is like your fingerprint, a unique mark in motion signifying who you are.

It can do all the talking for you.

A solid player is usually confident and comfortable. They know what an enhanced experience feels like, and they can consistently create it. Being in that state helps you play better, and a high-level player understands this fact. If you play with a sub-par player, the questions are: Are they open to the enhanced experience? Do they have a good attitude? And are they willing to learn? If they have a keen awareness of their surroundings and understand their playing partner's situation, they are on their way to being full-fledged grinders. If they are the type who is always mad when they hit a bad shot or talk in your backswing, they have a lot to learn.

A man's golf game and etiquette precede him, quite like his reputation.

As foursome friends, you are in the trenches together. You go through trials and tribulations, disappointment and excitement, laughter and pleasant surprise. You offer words of encouragement when they hit a good *or* bad shot. You accept their offer to help look for your ball. You share a beer and your course knowledge.

The entire scope of any human relationship is lived through the five-hour golf round. You tell jokes, discuss work, recount the serendipitous moment you met your significant other, and share stories of childhood. You may even sing songs together, all while playing the course and asking your partner to give you yardage on their rangefinder. You are there for each other—like soldiers at war, you become a band of brothers.

On the eighteenth green, you'll remove your hat and shake hands, and tell them it was a pleasure to play together. You depart as friends and, more often than not, never see each other again.

STOP AND SMELL THE ROSES

"As you walk down the fairway of life you must smell the roses, for you only get to play one round."
—Ben Hogan

A golf course is a finely manicured, beautiful slice of Earth. Why not use the natural elements around you to bring your game to a new level, de-stress, and refocus? All while staying present while enjoying your surroundings. Survey the area you are in, see what is growing naturally all around the course. Be in awe of the abundance of nature. Depending on where you live, you have a myriad of natural resources at your disposal.

Go pick some fresh lavender growing wild off the fairway, take a deep breath and inhale the fresh scent to calm your nerves before your next shot. Any fragrance you smell sends immediate signals to your limbic system, which is the "emotional center" of your brain. It helps regulate the nervous system, balance your mood, and relieve stress.

Use the pine pitch from a pine tree near the tee box, rub some on your left-hand palm to help your grip. Pick a lime off a tree and squeeze it into your water bottle. Feel free to pluck some rosemary or wild mint. Snatch a few lemons from the trees on the course—if your local climate allows, of course. Southern California has a ton of wild sage growing on most courses—take some home, use it to stuff your chicken for dinner that night.

There are infinite ways to stop and smell the roses. Sometimes, the key to your next shot is to not think about it. The secret to your swing is to keep your mind clear. Use nature to stay calm and remain grateful for these precious few hours of freedom you have to hit a white ball around an enormous green field.

Real-time aromatherapy is a trick to empty your head and appreciate the game you are playing. Absorb the elements which make it uniquely special—healing, even.

Mindful golf is grounded in gratitude. The appreciation for Gaia, Mother Earth, plays a major role in clearing your mind and playing well.

SECOND SHOT PRO

When I play with friends, they always bust my balls by calling me a "second shot pro." This means that after hitting a not-so-favorable first shot, I am known to pull a Quick Draw McGraw and reload. On my second swing, nine times out of ten, it goes where I meant for it to go the first time.

This can go for any shot, from a drive to a putt. As an example, while standing on a 182-yard par 3, the shot was just a standard 6-iron I've practiced a million times. I lined up, picked my target, and then—*snap*-hooked off the toe into a deep frontside bunker. *Not exactly* what I was trying to do.

Instead of a birdie putt, it will now take a stellar up and down just to save par. Disappointed and pissed off, I quickly teed it up, aimed, swung, and hit a bullet that ended up ten feet from the pin—which happens more often than not. *There's* the shot I've practiced a million times!

Second shot pro strikes again.

It is a frustrating lesson because (A) it proves I have the shot in my bag, and (B) it reminds me that I am still an amateur golfer. But the conundrum always remains: *Why did I not do that the first time?* I only score my first ball—to keep things fair, of course—but I hit the second shot for practice out of frustration. On the second attempt, the intention is to finish the swing with my hands, to end up on my left side and make sure I turn through the shot. Demonstrating a correct pass at the ball helps my confidence and allows me to move beyond the disappointment of that horrid first shot. It is a useful opportunity to create a better (muscle) memory.

When analyzing the difference in approach with the second go, two realizations occur: I take less than half the time in my pre-shot routine and just hit the shot. More doing, less thinking. The other realization is, I'm more relaxed on the second swing because I know it doesn't count. I lose the tightness in my grip and stop second-guessing. I don't get trapped in the cyclical routine of living in my head, thinking about anything *but* the swing I'm about to make.

The challenge is to be in the second shot mindset when hitting the first shot. It is a constant work in progress. We always want to play well, even though it may not be a tournament or a money game. That competitive spirit exists every time you grip a club. The lesson here is to not take on any unnecessary pressure. Just relax and release, put a swing on it, and let it fly!

None of us play well when we are frustrated or stressed. It all comes down to knowing thyself. You win under poise, not under pressure. Sometimes you are better off not giving a sh*t and just playing the game, especially when it's a non-competitive round for fun. The idea is to bring your range game to the course. If you can hit it purely and consistently on the range, you are more than capable of doing the same when you're playing eighteen.

It is all in your head. Finding your inner peace and Zen mind is paramount to success in not only golf, but in life. More trust, more flow. You can do this through simple breathing techniques, visualization, positive self-talk, or all of the above. Whatever works for you.

I cannot stress enough how much of a relief it is to pull a quick draw and get that better shot out of your system. I wholeheartedly believe that it helps your confidence to hit the right shot in real time. But you must do it quickly. If time allows and you're with the right crowd, drop another one, don't think, and hit a hellacious seed. It's a useful memory to draw from the next time you play—if you hit it well, of course. Forget the sh*tty shot, remember the good one.

In the long run, the better swing memory will count much more than any number you put down on your scorecard.

AIM SMALL

When you pick out your target and line up your club to the ball, be sure to use *two targets*: First, the one where you want your ball to go—and second, an intermediate target to be a point of reference right in front of you.

In the distance, where you are actually aiming, pick out the tiniest, specific target, like a cart path sign, a tree, a squirrel in the fairway, or anything your eye can missile-lock on. Find the smallest target you can see with your naked eye and zero in. Imagine a spotlight shining right at what you are seeing. The more acutely you aim, the more direct and accurate your shot will be.

A wide target is no good. Be as precise as possible. The more meticulous and specific you are, the better chance your ball will fly to the place you choose. Being precise gives your mind much less room for error. Your brain doesn't have to compute a large piece of data, such as fifty yards across an entire fairway. It can fixate on a smaller target with much more clarity.

Whether it's on the fairway or the green, once you find the specific spot you are targeting, identify the closer, intermediate target. It could be a leaf, a broken tee, a mark in the grass, or a yardage marker—anything about five feet in front of you that is in the direct line of your aiming point. It is a world easier to set up and accurately square the club to something directly ahead of you which is aligned with your ultimate target.

Now you are set up and prepared to pull the trigger. Your club is square with the intermediate target, and you are assured your aim is correct. There is no guesswork involved. Using this closer target simplifies your aim and will help you feel more confident you have it dialed in.

This is all about streamlining much of what can be intimidating to any golfer. You are looking to hit a small white ball hundreds of yards to a tiny, distant target. Bring the distance closer to you and feel the poise of a pro. This will result in a much higher chance you will hit the ball solidly where you want it to go. Any second-guessing you can eliminate will boost your game.

Approaching life is akin to this strategy. The sharper your focus, the clearer your desires become, making goal achievement more attainable.

Practice this time and again at the driving range. When you pick your target, place a tee about three to five feet in front of you. Acclimate yourself to using both targets to aim. This will not only improve your shot-making consistency but will increase your self-belief that your ball is going to fly right at your target.

You will feel a resolute certainty when lining up a shot. No more anxious hoping which results in shanks to the right or yanks to the left. More flush ball striking.

Your intention is to play good golf. In any round of golf, all your targets are their own small intentions within the larger objective of scoring better.

As you simplify the game, you give yourself easier access to more self-belief. More self-belief cultivates a more confident stroke, which will result in a better score and, of course, more fun.

YOUR GO-TO

Every great player has a pre-shot routine and uses it religiously, whether they are playing nine holes in a practice round or leading in the final round of The Masters. It is an indispensable aspect of staying present with each shot and an integral part of playing good golf. Creating this habit is essential for developing a consistent mental routine to help you when the pressure is on. Whatever it takes to feel comfortable over the ball—give yourself that extra bit of confidence.

The pre-shot routine helps you to think the same for every shot or putt, which simplifies your thoughts, creating a safe space for you to focus on the present. Your pre-shot routine is the foundation of your mental preparedness and toughness. It is the bubble you can live in which allows you to breathe, focus, and center yourself each and every time you hit or putt the ball.

Your routine should involve four main steps designed to bring together your analytical mind, your creativity, your emotions, and your athletic ability. The first happens in your left brain, your analytical mind. Size up the shot in front of you. The second is the right brain's turn to creatively visualize the shot shape you want to hit or the line of the putt you are seeing. The third is when you leave your mind and feel it with your body. It's where you rehearse the shot with practice swings (or strokes), imagining the end result. And the fourth is your execution—using your athletic ability for real-time manifestation. You implement in reality what you envisioned in your mind.

Broken down, here are your four key steps of the pre-shot routine:

1. *THINK:* Enter the Bubble

This is when you enter your bubble, focusing specifically on the shot or putt at hand. You are now standing behind the ball and analyzing what the plan of attack is, asking the questions:

- What is the best shot for this situation?
- What are the challenges (the golf course layout, weather conditions, your lie, etc.)?
- What is the risk-reward of each possible option and your confidence level with each?

2. *VISUALIZE:* Imagine Your Shot

Your focus is narrowed even more as you clearly see your target and imagine the flight of your ball and how it will bounce or roll.

For a putt, you see the line to the hole or spot to which you are aiming. Getting a feel for the optimal speed to get the ball in the cup—or at least close enough to leave you an easy tap in if you are just lagging it up there.

3. *FEEL*: Practice Swing Envisioning

You have decided on your shot and now rehearse it with practice swings. Time to waggle that sh*t.

This is where you *feel* the sensations of the shot you are about to hit and what will be etched in your brain when you step up to the ball. Now you are confident in your selection and 100 percent committed to the shot.

4. ***EXECUTE:* Engage and Trust**

You've analyzed your shot, rehearsed your swing, and are now set up to the ball, making certain your ball position is matched to the club you are using.

This is the time to:

- Quiet your mind.
- Stay connected to your target.
- Feel confident.
- Trust your swing.

Once you are in the execution phase, no thinking is necessary. It is all about being in a meditative, flow-type state where your mind is blank.

Your optimal state for performing any task is when no interference at all is coming from your analytical brain. No thinking. Your mind is an empty space wholly immersed in the activity. You are fully present—doing and being.

It is not always easy to find your flow-state—or "zone"—for each shot, but with this routine, you can give yourself those precious seconds required to focus and be the best you can be, one shot at a time.

These four steps of your go-to pre-shot routine can become a mindful exercise during your rounds and, quite frankly, a key performance indicator. Develop the routine that works for you, then practice until it becomes second nature. This means doing it every time you are at the range or even chipping balls in your yard. Training our mental game is just as important as training our golf swing.

SET THE TONE

Make things simple and easy for yourself before you play your next round: focus on your first tee shot. That is all. Your fundamental chief goal is to hit the golf ball in the fairway.

When you are on the tee, pick your specific target and intermediate target. Line up, commit, and swing easy. You don't need to hammer it. Go at it smoothly—as hard as you can while still keeping perfect balance. Find the fairway and hit your next shot from the short stuff. Again—*you do not need to hammer it!*

When you execute, you set the tone for your entire round. Psychologically, it's a boost of confidence to hit a good tee shot. It starts you off on the right foot, which makes playing much more fun. You're more likely to be telling stories and jokes when you're on the green staring at a birdie as opposed to looking for your ball in the woods.

"Just drop one, Todd!" you yell to your friend as you take a few practice strokes while he's still looking in the woods for his brand new Pro V1x.

Whether it's a tournament or you're going out with your buddies, keep it elementary. First shot is first. Your mindset is all about the number one tee, nothing else. Give yourself tunnel vision by taking it one shot at a time. Stay basic and keep the ball in front of you—a simple and effective strategy to manage expectations.

Setting the tone isn't limited to only hitting the driver on the range before you play. Of course, do your normal warm-up, go through your club progression wedges through woods. Play the first hole. Simulate the par 3s if you know the distances, the club, and the shape you want to play based on the day's wind.

Finish with a few drives on the range, release your hands, and turn through the ball. Swing with swagger. Find your tee shot tempo and walk to that tee box with a confident glide in your stride.

—THREE—

SOCIAL BUTTERFLY EFFECT

WHEN NOT TO TALK TO YOUR BUDDY

THE GAME OF GOLF IS HARD ENOUGH. The ups and downs during any round are not unlike the trials and tribulations of life itself. They are also not unlike the unavoidable circumstance after circumstance, where all you can do is play it where it lies and live with whatever is in front of you.

Golf puts a premium on *how* you play the game much more than *how well* you play the game. The game has its own unique etiquette, basic rules of acceptable behavior, from how one behaves on the greens to sharing a cart.

With golf cart etiquette, for instance, many factors are at play—*how* one drives the cart is of utmost importance. Things like parking protocol, avoiding obstruction or shadows, speed in finding the ball quickly, not wasting time circling, having a clear direction, and promptly locating. The more astute one is on these manners, the more enhanced the golf experience will be. This is a true definition of a "cartnership." There is a huge bonus for any golf cart partner who has an eagle eye and finds your ball before you do. For this reason, it's always a treat to play with anyone who's been a caddy—as well as for the stories.

All the while, the game is being played. There are definitely times when you really do not want to talk, listen, or care about anything but your next shot. It is true golf etiquette to know when you need to shut up while your buddy processes that he yanked his brand new TaylorMade 5-wood into the water with 215 to the pin. He hit a bomb off the tee, now he's in the drink. There is nothing you can say at that moment that will make *anything* better.

When appropriate, remind him that it's seventy-eight degrees and you are out swinging the club with beautiful scenery. More often than not, though, you need to just shut your mouth to help him focus on the next swing. Any competitor knows the vibe—that moment of true tension seconds after your partner hits a bad shot. Any athletic person who has a competitive inner fire understands that edge between playing good and playing great—the desire to get better and the will to win. That competitive spirit only makes one more pissed when a shot goes awry. When your buddy shanks his shot and gets in the cart, that is the time when there is nothing to say. Silence is golden.

Conversely, when *you* hit a dismal shot, have the self-awareness to limit any self-indulgent moping or hoping, bitching or moaning, recounting how the lie was the problem or how that shot should be super-easy for you. One, two comments max, and move on to the next shot. If you need to self-indulge, ask permission to take five to fifteen seconds of grumbling time and get it all out. Your golf buddy doesn't need to hear the complaining while he has his own issues to deal with, like a tricky 172-yard shot from a fairway bunker.

Also, don't be adding your strokes out loud while your partner is still standing over his putt. I once had a guy ask me if he got a 7 or 8 while I was lining up an eagle putt on a long par 5. I just absolutely nuked a 250-yard 3-wood over water and had a nice ten-footer for a 3. Count your own score, have a Coke and a smile, and know when to shut the f*%k up.

Of course, there are plenty of times when chatter is welcome. Sometimes you need to take your mind off the game and just enjoy the company. It is up to your level of awareness and empathy to know when to do either. Listening to a funny story on the way to a tee box is a fantastic way to reset your mind. Changing the subject usually results in a more relaxed feeling and an easier, smoother swing.

The game of golf is a true test of the entire human condition. Riding the wave of a golf round is an athletic, emotional experience with a social twist.

When all three click, you have the kind of addictive experience to keep you coming back. Every golfer—from chop to pro—knows the feeling.

Either way, no matter how competitive and serious you are about golf, it *is* a game. Have a good walk, don't be a whiny b*tch, and know some good jokes.

DO YOU SPEAK RANGE?

If you are at the driving range and see someone smoking balls straight and consistently, don't be shy—be social and engage them in conversation. We've all been there. Golfers *love* to talk about their own game.

Ask them about ball position when they hit their wedges compared to their long irons and fairway woods. Inquire about anything you're working on at that time, as they may in fact have an insight you never thought of or may share a little piece of knowledge that will make the difference the next time you play.

Be brave. Dare to ask them to give you a fifteen-second look at your swing while you hit a ball. This does two things for you: First, it gives you real-time feedback from a respectable golfer, and second, it applies some pressure as you to execute the shot. If things align well, it may even get you into a memorable conversation. You cannot underestimate the value of having a second pair of eyes watch your swing.

There is nothing like simulating the nerves of hitting a golf shot in front of people.

The scene looks like this: You are hitting balls at the range and you notice a dude of similar age having a solid sesh. He's clearly a player and hits a pretty consistent ball. As he walks by your hitting zone, you time it out, the double Dutch stagger, waiting for the right moment, trying to minimize the awkwardness.

You meet eyes and yell, "Hey partner, you mind if I get thirty seconds—take a look at my swing?"

Your stomach hits your throat, you know it's a somewhat unusual ask. After all, he was just minding his business.

He gladly obliges, "Hell yeah, man. Give it a rip."

Relieved and excited, you get into mode, doing all the things the pros do: the pre-shot routine, a deep breath, set up, and pipe your 3-wood toward the 200-yard flag.

He says, "Nice. Where do you play?"

You tell him how you play all over—mostly the county courses and occasional private club. He tells you he belongs to the country club down the street as you chatter on about your games and the local courses. It turns out you both have friends in common and your wives went to school together. He's also a big Real Madrid fan and you respect anyone who digs European football. You exchange Instagram handles, then he drops how he needs a fourth next Saturday. You gladly accept and now have a Saturday tee time at a sweet country club with your new golf buddy.

It's worth the ask. You never know. Get out of your comfort zone and make some new friends.

Use the time at the range in a creative way. Simulate that pressure you'll feel on the first tee next Saturday. Hit a mindful bucket. Be aware of the elements around you, especially the other players putting *their* time in the dirt.

A WORD TO THE WISE IS ENOUGH

Try listening to the old guys talking in the pro shop. You can gain an infinite amount of knowledge from listening to others who love the game as much as you do. A lot can be learned from those who have played the game more years than you've been alive.

This is all about using your playing and practice time with more purpose.

Think like a consummate student and be sociable. If you are at the course café and you overhear any of those old-timers telling tales from their golf days of old, explaining how they grip the club, or telling the story about their first hole-in-one, do yourself a favor and take mental notes.

So much hidden knowledge can be ascertained by simply engaging in conversation with fellow golf enthusiasts, even those guys who hang around the course talking everyone up who will listen. You know who that is, every course has one—they all look and sound like Morgan Freeman. That dude is literally *begging* to share his knowledge. Be the one to absorb it all like a sponge. Ask questions, show him your swing, buy him a beer.

The stories may not just be entertaining, they may improve your game. You never know where an insanely profound tip is going to drop from. At the very least, it's something to think about on your drive home, or even during your next range session. Always be on the lookout for knowledge.

Golf is a social game, and socialization takes place on the course *but primarily* off the course. Think about it: You spend most

of your time *not* golfing—even if we all wish this was different. Besides your career, kids, and other life responsibilities, the reality is you have plenty of time to talk golf between rounds.

If you are obsessed—like many of us are—then you are constantly thinking about your last best shot, or your 9:00 a.m. tee time this upcoming Saturday. Maybe you're smiling right now because you know it's true.

Golf is an intellectual game. It always helps your shot-making when you can apply some philosophy behind it.

The more you listen and learn, the better you will be.

GOOD ONES COUNT

If you consider yourself a sub-par golfer and know there's no way in hell you're shooting under 95 or 100, then don't pay much attention to the score at all. Look at it as secondary. Instead, keep note of your finest swings and the best shots you hit during the round. In essence, you are playing two games: the actual game of golf where strokes count, and your self-improvement game where you are evaluating how well you play by the number of worthy swings you put on the ball.

Score your good shots, forget your strokes. If you make five great swings in a round, that's what you want to commit to memory. Go over those moments in your head continuously. If you can have seven excellent swings the next round, and ten the next, then you are making progress. This memory game will give you inspiration as a player.

For example, if you take a snowman (8) on a hole, but you hit a great second shot, make note of it. Take the positive from the hole. The other seven shots may have sucked, but who cares about the number on the scorecard when you are learning the game? Stay focused and keep score of all your quality swings. You know, the times when the ball *actually* goes where you aim. Your swing feels fluid and you get that *feeling* you're always looking for when you practice. I guarantee that is what you'll remember most—and it's what you *should* remember most when you look back at your round.

Save your scorecards for reference. Record your notes on the holes where you make the good swings (or putts) to trigger your memory. It is very difficult to recall all of your shots, but if you annotate the ones you hit well on the actual holes, you can use those as fuel for the next time you play. There isn't much room in those little squares on the scorecards, so you can use a simplistic code system to remind yourself what you did: U/D for up and down, G/C for a good chip, G/D for a great drive, A/5i for awesome 5-iron, and so on. Develop a system which succinctly reminds you what you'd like to remember. How you do it is up to you.

If you are playing with a foursome and don't have room on the card, grab yourself a second card and make your own notes on it. Take this "note card" home with you and study it after your round. When you remember those good shots, you'll enjoy the round a second time because you know the score doesn't matter, only the good shots do. It's all about building confidence, brick by brick, shot by shot, while you become a better player.

Taking the positive from any situation is a useful tool in any walk of life, but especially when you are learning the game of golf. Who gives a crap what your final score is? Remember what you did well and build on it for next time.

PREP IN YOUR STEP

Let's say you have a round set for the weekend. Your golf friends are texting on a group chat, the chatter starts during the week, and as the days go by, the excitement builds.

Golf is a highly technical game with a hundred variables. Getting a grip on the variables you can control makes a huge difference in not only *how* you play but how much you enjoy playing. Here is a simple checklist for you to use in the days before—and during—your round.

PREP STEPS

Your Mind

1. ***Mental Preparation***
    - Watch golf. Start your mental diet right and remind yourself of how the greatest play the game. Take mental notes of their swings and practice in the mirror.

- Assume you will play your best.
- Journal and script out your round.

2. ***Course Strategy***
    - If you know the course already, you can play it in your head.
    - If you are playing somewhere new, look online at the layout and get a sense of how your game fits the track and how you can play each hole.

Playing and Practicing

3. ***Swing the Club***
    - If you have time, go to the range. Hit a bucket and spend time chipping.
    - If you have less time, warm up at home by swinging in your backyard or your living room. Chip wiffle balls. Practice putting on your rug.

Maintenance

4. ***Clean and Mark***
    - Use soap and water to get your clubs shiny and ready.
    - Mark the balls you'll be playing with. One of the best ways to mark is to use a line to help you aim putts and tee shots alike.

Day Before

5. ***Plan the Route***
    - Map out the best route to the course.
    - Pack the car the night before, if possible.
    - Leave early before your tee time, so you have no stress while driving.

6. ***Meal Prep***
    - Prepare any snacks, pack your lunch, and bring drinks, depending on what time of day you are playing. Make sure you have the right nutrition and stay hydrated. A Gatorade and banana are a good start.

7. ***Good Night's Sleep***
    - Make sure you are well-rested. Go to bed early and start dreaming of hitting great shots.

At the Course

8. ***Warm Up***
    - Stretch and get limber before you swing any club. Your body is your temple and the more warmed up you are, the better you will feel and the less chance of injury.

9. ***Stretch While You Play***
    - People always talk about warming up before your round, but please remember to keep loose during your

round. You can stretch while waiting to tee off or when there are a few minutes between swings.

10. ***Hit Balls***
    - Warm up on the range by starting with wedges and working your way up through the bag. If you don't have time to hit every club, at least hit a wedge, short iron, mid-iron, and driver or fairway wood. Find out what your ball is doing that day. Treat the last few shots as you would the first hole or two of the course you are playing.

11. ***Short Game***
    - Chip and putt before teeing off. If you have less time, you can chip a few on the range.
    - For putting, if you want to get a feel for the greens, take three balls and do some one-handed long putts to get an idea of the speed.

12. ***Have Fun***
    - Forget scoring and focus on one shot at a time. You've done all the preparation, now it's time to enjoy the moment. The more fun you have, the better you play. It's funny how it works that way.

PITCH AND PUTT

Spend time around the green.

When teaching first-time golfers, Harvey Penick started people at the hole. He preached the value of learning the "unteachable" qualities of *touch* and *feel.* Getting comfortable from the hole out will automatically make you a better player. Take a ball and putter and start six inches from the hole, make the putt, then back up a foot. Make that one. Then back up again.

If you are new to golf, the number one thing to do is to get a feel for the short game. Learn the putting stroke, get a feel for lag putting, master the chipping stroke. I know it's tempting to bomb drivers all day. But chipping and putting for hours around the green is way more valuable as more than half of your strokes come from within one hundred yards.

It is essential to keep variety in your practice routine to help keep you engaged and attentive. Play games as a way to structure your training time. Use the drills to add an element of competition and up the pressure a bit. Challenge your practice buddy and play for a prize. If you have something at stake, it gives you the extra bit of concentration needed to get the ball in the hole.

Par 2s is an effective drill when you are on a practice green. Pick out a random hole from where you are standing. Get up and down in two, or better yet, try for the ace. Practice your lag putting, practice short and medium putts. The lowest score wins. Play nine different holes, or eighteen, or as many as you wish.

You can also play Par 2s with wedges. Pick a hole and chip

toward it. Finish with a putter. Mix it up and practice a variety of shots around the green from different lies. Give yourself a chance: get your ball rolling to the target, weight on your front foot, descending blow, no more chunk duffs. Get up and down. Playing one ball into the hole keeps you focused like you are in a match.

Practice on and around the green. Chip, pitch, and putt. Hit from the bunker. Always have a target. Play for something. The more you can simulate real-life circumstances, the more you'll be able to step up when it counts.

If you are looking to shave three to five strokes off your score, the quickest way is to dedicate 90 percent of your practice time to chipping and putting. Find the technique that is repeatable for you and commit. Short game mastery will lower your score and make you a better ball striker. Make it fun, get a consistent click off the clubface, and watch a few roll in the cup.

— FOUR —
WHAT'S OLD IS NEW

STOIC HEROICS

BEAUTY LIES IN THE EXCELLENCE OF OUR MINDS AND CHARACTER. When considering the essence of Stoicism, it is important to remember that the Stoics thought of philosophy as a way to live by virtue, or as Cicero put it, *summum bonum*, "the highest good." It's what we all should be aiming for in this life. Virtue refers to mastering your own character and applying reason in a manner that's healthy and respectable.

The four virtues of Stoicism are *courage, temperance, justice,* and *wisdom.* Their teachings remind us that we don't control external events, but we *do* control how we deal. In other words, it's not what happens to us, but our reactions that matter.

Adapting this philosophy into your golf game will reduce your stress levels and serve as a reminder that it is *how* you play the game which really matters, not exactly *how well.* Keep your mind serene and clear. Focus only on what's in your control and choose reason over emotion.

Be a stoic golfer. Having this mental fortitude will keep you more prepared to deal with anything life and golf throws at you. Play the best golf of your life.

Here are five ways to be a Stoic with a club in your hand:

1. ***Question yourself: "Is this within my control?"***

"Make the best use of what is in your power, and take the rest as it happens. Some things are up to us, and some things are not up to us."

—Epictetus

This is otherwise known as the dichotomy of control: what you can control are your thoughts and actions, what you cannot control is everything else. The most important practice in Stoic philosophy is differentiating what you have influence over and what you do not. From this understanding, you then focus only on what is in your control.

In golf, you can control the equipment you use, how often (and well) you practice, your swing, and your attitude. That is it. The rest is not up to you at all. Yes, practicing often can affect your chances of playing better, but you can never account for the wind, course conditions, a bad break, or your opponent when playing competitively.

Like Epictetus says, we spend our time foolishly if we waste it worrying about the things that are not up to us. This is a lesson in acceptance and a map to a place of peace. This alone can alleviate so much suffering from both our lives and our golf game. Do your best and accept what is.

2. ***Avoid labeling anything "Good" and "Bad."***

"A wise man dyes events with his own color."

—Seneca

Don't judge the moment. Find the opportunity in adversity. Move on from your mistakes or your bad shots. No amount of anger or complaining can bring the past back to the present. Seneca also says, "There's nothing either good or bad but thinking makes it so."

Use any unfavorable situation as an opportunity to remain in control of what and how you think. Don't be fragile if things seemingly aren't going your way. Your mind will spin out of control if you let it. View the situation as it is, with no point of view. Your perception can be controlled. Take your opinion out of it and refrain from overreacting or getting too emotional. Stay even-keeled, don't give a sh*t either way. Swing your swing.

3. ***Memento Mori: "Remember, you must die."***

"You can leave right now, let that determine what you say or think."

—Marcus Aurelius

Whether you are practicing on the range or competing in a tournament, always keep in mind that you have a choice to make in each moment. You can make your time valuable by allowing it to bring you closer to a set goal or count towards your overall progress. Or you can waste your time with short-term pleasure and a bad attitude. It is entirely up to you. But what is not up to you is the ticking clock. The time passes and you will never get it back.

We only have our current swing—that is it. Every shot in every round consists of a singular swing after swing. We must enjoy our time and treat it with the utmost reverence. Your time on the golf course called Earth is finite. Do not waste any of it.

4. ***Practice negative visualization.***

"He robs present ills of their power who has perceived their coming beforehand."

—Seneca

We all practice negative visualization in the form of prevention. Preventive actions like buying health insurance, installing an alarm system in your house, or bringing extra golf balls in your bag are all common ways we prepare for possible mishaps. And no matter how much we prepare, bad breaks are an inevitable reality.

That is why Seneca says when we think about these things beforehand, it will minimize their impact if they actually happen. No matter how many preventative measures we put in place, we have zero control over whether they come to fruition. The person who expects nothing but good fortune is setting themselves up for massive disappointment. Preparing for misfortune while keeping a positive mental attitude is the sweet spot in living harmoniously.

This voluntary discomfort helps you manage your reactions to that bad drive or lip-out putt for par. The more you can visualize discomfort, the easier it is to deal with. On your way to the course, imagine hitting recovery shots. Prepare on the range, take a few balls, and practice swings you may need if things go awry.

5. ***Amor Fati: "Love of Fate."***

> "Love the hand that fate deals you and play it as your own, for what could be more fitting?"
>
> —Marcus Aurelius

Do not waste a second being pissed off about a bad lie or any misfortune, as whatever you are facing is meant to be overcome.

You have no choice—play it as it is. If your emotions do get the best of you, give yourself ten to fifteen seconds to get yourself together, then walk through the gate of regret and prepare for your next swing. Just enjoy the game. You have another chance to write another story.

Treat challenges as something to be embraced, not avoided. All things happen for a reason. It is up to you to paint that reason as a positive, thus more useful for you and your growth as a player *and* as a human being. Stay in reality and take it as it is. There is no need to create unnecessary suffering by creating a false meaning to what you experience, like telling yourself you suck after a terrible shot or stewing over a bad break for longer than necessary.

> "If it's endurable, then endure it. Stop complaining."
> —Marcus Aurelius

Play your golf as a Stoic.

The Stoics teach us how to keep a calm, rational mind no matter what happens, guiding us to focus only on what is within our own power. Beyond our personal thoughts, judgments, and actions, everything else in life is *not* up to us. We might as well lean into what we *can* control and surrender to the rest.

The ultimate beauty in how you play and live lies in your character: living by virtue and embracing what is in front of you at all times. Imagine what Marcus Aurelius would do if his ball landed in a divot or if he 3-putted from ten feet? He said, "You have power over your mind—not outside events. Realize this and you will find strength."

The quality of your thoughts determines the quality of your life—and how you're going to play. You will always be as good as your mindset.

Muhammad Ali said, "I am the greatest. I said that even before I knew I was."[1]

Conquer the low-vibrational thoughts of regret and anguish and you'll come out the other end happier and fulfilled. Those negative thoughts can and will cross your mind—let them pass, then adapt and overcome.

DON'T JUDGE THE MOMENT

I've been there a million times. The big, "Oh, f*ck" moment after blowing a drive *way* right and then having to look for the ball for ten minutes. Yes, it's truly annoying and very easy for an amateur golfer to lose interest in the hole after such a momentum killer. It's easy to circle the cart back and forth, so pissed you find it impossible to concentrate on the next shot whether you find the ball or not. Very often, this hiccup affects your next swing—and maybe even the next.

We are over-analytical human thinkers who tend to label everything as "good" or "bad." Think about it: we filter everything through the question, "Is this good or is this bad…?"

We create limitations the minute we label something. These labels usually stick in our minds. Once we put it in a category, it's extremely difficult to change it into anything else. The reality is nothing is either good *or* bad—it is all a matter of perception. The key is to be fluid and remain in the moment. Everything is an illusion—things are not always what they seem at first.

Take any golf shot you hit. Where your ball ends up is all that matters. Like those times when you are staring down your target and committing to a shot shape, then you swing and end up hitting a skiddlydank wormburner that runs along the ground and miraculously ends up where you were aiming. You didn't exactly draw it up like that, but it's right where you want it to be. Of course, we all want to hit beautiful shots with every swing, but the final score on the card is just a number. Anyone would take an ugly par over a beautiful bogey.

It is best to stay free of judgment. You never know when your next lucky break will come. And why put more pressure on yourself? The only thing you can do within your control is to put your best move on the ball, hit it as purely as you can, and hope for the best. This goes for any level player. Sometimes it's better to be lucky than good.

The minute you label a golf shot as "not favorable," you lose the opportunity to see the positive. Just *being able to hit a golf shot* is a blessing in itself. Stay in the present, enjoy your time. Use the moment as an opportunity to add value to your life. Don't judge yourself or others—and especially do not judge your next stroke.

Okay, you may have hit an embarrassing slice with your 3-iron on that long par 3, but chances are it's at least closer to the hole. Even if you are left in tough rough or behind a tree, bring out your inner Tiger and figure it out.

You are always one shot away from glory.

THE PRESS

My grandfather, John J. Rota, always preached the advantages of playing golf with a press. He emphasized playing the ball off your back foot, closing the clubface, and having more of a bump and run mentality, where you hit a low draw into the green and let it run out. He would say to keep your hands in front of the ball, a crucial best practice for any effective golf swing.

As a youth, I adapted this right-to-left shot shape to my iron play. It trained me to keep my hands ahead of the ball and get the compression, the most out of every shot with a draw—a right-to-left shot that would roll for days. The drive would be in the air for what seemed like minutes, then land and roll out another thirty yards. I got very used to out-driving all my friends—*and* my dad's colleagues when he brought me out on company outings.

This critical piece of information passed on by my grandfather gave me a vision: I saw my game in the shape of right-to-left. This is a simple skill that allowed me to focus and hone my aim. I was able to understand my ball flight distinctly hitting the trap draw all day long. That was all I needed to know. When I practiced, I always aimed right and played the right-to-left shot toward each target.

As I got older and my game improved, my ball position varied. Instead of a trap draw, I began to move the ball forward in my stance. As Tom Watson advocates, "The hitting zone is from the middle of the stance forward."[2] When I moved my ball position up in my stance, my ball flight went straighter and higher (as opposed to always a stinging right-to-left draw). This is a much more controllable ball flight and has allowed me to play and score more consistently. Yes, I still hit a draw since it's my natural ball flight, though more by choice than by default.

There are so many unknown factors in the game of golf. If you can zero in on your tendencies in ball flight, that known factor will be an essential accelerator in helping you to shoot lower rounds consistently. When you are practicing at the range, notice how your ball travels. What is your natural ball shape? Find out, then zero in more acutely on your shot visualization. Paying closer attention to this is a tiny action you can take to improve.

At the range, don't just hit and hit and tire yourself out without any real point. Pick a target every shot and notice how your ball moves in the air. You may be a left-to-right player. If you hit that fade consistently, you can more easily predict where your shot will end up. This can take a lot of guesswork out of your game when you play a round. If you don't get to practice very often, get the most out of your range time and make use of every ball you strike. Make every swing count. Find your game.

Do whatever makes the game easier for you. For me, playing it off my back foot with a press made the game simpler and allowed me to cover the ball more consistently. I very rarely hit a slice. It also became an amazingly efficient way to deal with trouble shots and chipping just off the green.

To practice trouble shots, my grandfather used to put a ball under a tree and position me halfway under the branches, using an 8- or 9-iron, press off my back foot with weight on my left. With just a simple up-and-down motion, the ball would shoot out underneath a branch and roll right up the lip of the green. It is a nice "get out of jail" golf shot to have in your bag. Because the loft of the club is lowered, the ball rockets off the clubface like it's a 5-iron and can roll out through the rough, through the fringe and onto the green with more ease. Any amateur will be well-served to have this shot as part of their repertoire.

If you miss the green and have a short chip to the pin—with green to work with—the bump and run is the most high-percentage shot you can use to get the ball rolling toward your target. Think of it as just a putt with your wedge—simple as that. When you play with a press, you are lowering the loft of the club. A straightforward back-and-forth motion, hands ahead of the ball, brushing the grass. No need to break your wrist. Hinge and hold. Being consistent when chipping just off the green makes a huge difference in shooting a lower score. Half the battle is your follow-through and getting the ball going toward the target. Give yourself a chance.

Two big keys to remember are the start and the finish of the pendulum. The start: The height of your backswing should match the height of your follow-through. Oftentimes, an amateur player chunks it because they decelerate on their follow-through, especially when they chip. They have a big backswing and a sudden stop as they hit *at* the ball rather than *through* it.

The finish: When chipping, your weight should be distributed more on your left foot (if you are right-handed). Balancing 65 percent of your weight on your front foot is the way to get through the ball and finish on your left side. When you watch a tour pro swing, they always get to their left side.

With all the technology out there, sometimes it pays to keep it "old school."

Ben Hogan himself preferred to play low chip shots as he felt they were much easier to control. He preached having your hands ahead of the ball, keeping them low through impact. Minimizing any hand movement keeps impact solid and consistent and helps you avoid scooping the ball. Hinge and hold.

The more consistent play is the play with the least moving parts. When you chip, keep it fundamental, hands ahead of the ball, have your weight on your front foot, and finish each shot.

HIT THE OLD CLUBS

"Some of the players doing well now, if you gave them a persimmon wood they wouldn't be able to get the ball off the ground."[3]

—Miguel Ángel Jiménez

Notice the footwork of the old-timers—they danced on the ball in a different way. Those persimmon drivers require more knee bend and a soupy, wristy waggle-type swing. They require you to stay down on the ball and finish. They force you to be more fundamentally sound since the old clubs lack the extreme forgiveness of what we use today. If you can hit those clubs well, you are loose and letting your hands flow through the ball. It's a good idea to get accustomed to how the pioneers of golf felt when the ball met the club.

The earliest shafts were made of ash and other local European woods. When golf arrived in America in the 1800s, hickory shafts became the standard material. These newer woods had increased durability and were a bit more consistent, but because of the torque of the hickory, you had to have good wrist action at impact to stay on-line. A player had to keep them waggly to get the ball in the air—otherwise, it was slice and chase all day. Steel was introduced in 1925 and became the standard in the 30s.

Practicing with the old irons and woods makes you realize how hard the game of golf is and how amazingly fantastic the old-timers were at ball striking. The old pros had to hit all kinds of shots. They were forced to play with much more imagination. The way the swing has evolved in today's game is more technical, more rigid—less feely-soupy-waggly.

Hitting the old clubs is a bit different. You have to add more swivel in your wrist and learn some new dance moves with your feet and knees. When you return to your own modern sticks, watch the difference in how you can adapt the old school swing to modern technology. Notice the hinge in your wrist as you take the club back, the feeling of fluidity as you strike the ball then turf. The technology in today's clubs (especially shafts) is much different, but the liquidness you adopt in your motion when you learn to hit the older clubs applies and will help you relax into your swing. It also trains your hand-eye coordination to hit it off the sweet spot more often. Swing with natural rhythm. Get that mash compression feel.

I have a fifty-year-old 1-iron that I practice with once in a while. It's a Wilson Staff blade, about an inch and a half in height, steel shaft, original taped grip, no loft. Hitting that club is an accomplishment in itself. Every missed shot is pronounced—there is no forgiveness. The sting in my hands when making contact with the 1-iron is like fouling an inside pitch off with an aluminum bat. It's very difficult to hit a straight ball off that clubface, which is why it's effective to practice with it from time to time. I keep my angles tight, trying to keep the club under control. It's a fight, like reeling in a two-hundred-pound marlin off the Florida Keys. When I go back to my contemporary clubs, they feel so unbelievably buttery, if not magical.

Before club makers invested millions of dollars looking to push technology by hiring top engineers from the aerospace industry to design and manufacture NASA-level equipment, there were actually minimal choices in golf clubs and their performance. Today, irons and woods are developed using state-of-the-art computer technology composed of Space Age materials like titanium, graphite, and zirconia. But prior to the technological boom, people bought new clubs because their old ones wore out, not because of new titanium clubface technology or a lighter, more flexible shaft.

Technology mattered less in those days—which is what's so cool about playing with the old sticks. They're a great equalizer. You have to put a real swing on one to see it work for you. You don't have the technology to lean on to hide the flaws in your swing. Hitting the ball in the center of the clubface is at a premium. With the old clubs, you literally have to hit the ball on the screws. The sweet spot is minuscule, and you are fully exposed.

The PGA Tour should host one event a year where the players use the old clubs—it would be a delight for all fans. How fun would it be to see Rory McIlroy hit a persimmon driver, or Viktor Hovland hit an old blade iron? It would be interesting to see who would emerge as the champion because more flaws would be revealed when hitting the old clubs. Would this even out the field, or would the top players still emerge? Every player out there would have to adjust their game.

If you have access to old woods or irons, take them to the range once in a while. Get the feel of old-school golf. Summon the spirits of golfers past. Those souls paved the way for all of us to bomb 300-yard drives on any given Saturday, using Titleist Pro Vs and their penetrating trajectory and TaylorMade Qi10 drivers with inertia-powered forgiveness.

Appreciate and master the little things.

Appreciate and master the little things like footwork, where your hands are set at the top, the follow-through, your wrist action, and balance—and how the ball feels when it compresses against the center of the clubface.

Sometimes I wonder how Bobby Jones or Walter Hagen would have played using state of the art Honma irons with modern forged construction in a beautiful muscle back design. My guess is they'd play pretty damn well.

THE DEVIL'S IN THE DETAILS

Attention to small details makes the biggest difference. Thoroughness and thoughtfulness toward your craft will give you a competitive edge. Most people don't bother going the extra mile. People are conditioned to overlook and generalize to keep things simple and easy. However, when you do put in the time to dig deeper, you are intentionally stepping up your game.

First and foremost: You cannot fine-tune your swing and lower your score at the same time. Doesn't work. You have to compartmentalize your time. When you practice, think technical, be methodical, and do your drills. When you play, hit your shots and stay present. Let go of theory and swing with freedom.

You can add value to your game by understanding the nuanced little details within your control, and then optimize that knowledge. Here are some foundational details you can incorporate to lower your score:

1. ***Develop a Swing Platform***

Position, grip, stance, aim, and posture dictate all action. The elite player has excellent posture and is consistent in their setup. You can develop a pro-style setup as well. Swing your clubs at home, watch golf swings online, consult a coach. Your swing platform and ball position are priority.

2. *Know Your Bag*

Understand your equipment. Spend enough time on the range to know your distances. Play with clubs long enough to get used to a specific feel. Swapping out too often does you a disservice if you're looking to score lower. Stick with one ball. Just like your irons, the feel of the ball will help you get tuned in to your distances and—very importantly—your feel around the greens.

3. *Take More Club*

It's all tempo and balance—no need to swing ferociously. Know your distances. Use the technology available. Hit balls, shot-track, and dial in your numbers. If you need extra distance, just club up. This is especially relevant in a tough wind. When it's blowing in, use more club. And when it's downwind, club down. Shape your shots with the way the wind is blowing—draw and fade the ball with the given elements.

4. *Drain Six-Footers*

Consistent putting within six feet is a shortcut to lowering your score. If your number one priority is shaving strokes, spend time putting! Think about (1) your blade aim at impact and (2) speed.

5. *Have a Favorite Wedge*

Pick a go-to loft when you chip. Get the feel with that wedge everywhere around the greens. Develop stock shots using the length of backswing only. Lock in on your distance control with all wedges. When you know exactly how far you hit your favorite wedge, you will hit more greens and chip closer to more pins.

6. ***Know Thyself***
Know your body and what it's capable of doing. Understand your game and play to your strengths. Keep within yourself and avoid comparison with other players. We all have our unique swings and approaches. Stay in your lane. Put the time in and turn your limitations into strengths.

We all come back to center in our own way. A meticulous understanding of your swing, your unique approach to the game, and your physical capabilities are your competitive edge. Trust your instincts and be confident you are improving each time. Always look for a new detail that keeps you steps ahead of the competition.

Heightened awareness and attention to detail will put you well beyond the average player. Focusing on the details others do not see will be the difference between victory and defeat.

WHEN PLAY IS SLOW, PLAY TENNIS

I get it—you're playing your local muni on a Saturday and you have to wait fifteen minutes per hole to tee off. Then another fifteen for the green to clear. Instead of getting frustrated and losing your rhythm, grab a couple of balls, and find room either on another tee box or in a clear opening. Have your golf buddy stay in another area and chip back and forth with each other. Landing the ball safely in front of his feet, allow it to roll up perfectly for him to pick up and chip back to you.

Do this for a couple of rounds until it's time to hit. One of you can even play wide receiver and quarterback—chipping to a spot for the other to catch. Run some fifty or sixty-yard post patterns to the end zone . . . or golf cart.

If you skull one thin and it happens to hit the cart of the foursome on the hole behind you, hide your club fast and pretend it wasn't you. Maybe blame your partner. You never saw a thing.

You will be surprised when you have that exact shot on the same hole. I cannot tell you how many times this has happened to me—waiting on the tee box, chipping forty yards to my friend as we wait. Just a nice, rhythmic pitch back and forth. Sure enough, ten minutes later, I am left with a thirty-six-yard pitch shot to a back-pin position. Luckily, I had practiced this fifty times only minutes before. Muscle memory is the name of the game with your short approaches.

Chipping back and forth keeps you warm and gives you that extra bit of practice while playing. This is not a Tour event, so do this at your own risk—and only if there is time and room.

It is highly recommended to keep in motion while you wait.

— FIVE —
PRESENCE PRESENTS

PRESENT TENSE

TO PLAY RESPECTABLE GOLF, YOUR PRESENCE IS REQUIRED. To be present is the only way to genuinely express yourself and find the true uniqueness of your golf swing. Finding your swing simply means figuring out what works best for you. This is a key to unlocking your full grinder potential.

No sport has so much time between action. A player has almost too much time to think in between shots, making it super-easy to get lost in their own head. In other sports you don't have as much time to think; it's all reactionary as the action ebbs and flows from millisecond to millisecond.

The main block to any free swing is getting stuck in the methodical routine. I love how the legendary Bruce Lee defines this: "When one is not expressing himself, he is not free. Thus he begins to struggle, and the struggle breeds *methodical routine.*

Pretty soon on, [he] is doing his methodical routine as a response rather than responding to what is."[1]

In other words, the methodical routine is composed of your thoughts and behaviors based on past conditioning. You know the drill: You step to your ball, set up, look at your target, then . . . you second-guess your grip, ponder what the guys on the range told you, remember what you heard on *Playing Lessons With the Pros* the night before . . . You let your mind run amok. Your heart beats faster, your palms sweat, and you're psyching yourself out.

If that's you, you're stuck in the methodical routine. In your head, overthinking, living in yesterday. Doing everything but paying attention to what is right in front of you. Next time this happens, take a mental note of it. Then forget everything. Go blank. Step away. Run through your pre-shot routine again. Playing good golf demands you to stay in the *now*.

Step behind the ball and look at your target from the vantage point of the ball itself. Think about what you are looking to do and where you want to go at that exact moment. Close your eyes if it helps: visualize the feel of the shot, how the ball is going to soar in the air. Envision the end result. Free your mind. Then take a deep breath and put your move on it. Release the club and don't hold back!

Every golf shot requires you to be present and execute what you've practiced and committed to muscle memory. The only way to hit a good golf shot is to empty your mind. The only way to empty your mind is to recognize when you're in the methodical routine. Step away, breathe, and revisit.

Let go and just play. Better yet, forget you are playing and just *be*.

MONKEY CROSSING

Playing golf in Asia is just different.

The East is the first to greet the sun, and I think that has a say in how the East influences culture, from innovative thinking, to new technology, to fashion. The first daylight sunrise belongs to Asia-Pacific (APAC). The people, places, and things have a completely different mindset than the West, and I love it.

To play golf in Singapore isn't that convenient for the average player. You literally need to take a one-hour ferry to Indonesia to play a round. Yes, there are city tracks in Singapore, but their ranges are unnecessarily expensive, and you are forced to hit off mats. Going to Indo, golf is way more luxurious. There are two main islands off the coast of Singapore to play golf—Batam and Bintan. Bintan is the more upper-class version of a golf trip, weekend-type place with resorts and white sand beaches. Batam is a bit more debauchery, strip club, bachelor(ette) party style, with a few good tracks.

I became good friends with Mark, the manager of the building in Clarke Quay, the area of Singapore where I was living. We always talked golf, and eventually, Mark set up a round to play with a few of his friends. He lent me a set of Wilson blades to use, with a couple of TaylorMade fairway woods.

We played Legends Golf & Country Resort, a Jack Nicklaus-designed course in Johor, Malaysia. We left at 5:00 a.m. and crossed the border in Mark's Benz. The track was tricky and under-kept, but incredibly beautiful, with danger everywhere.

There was crazy intense humidity and full forests of naturally growing palm trees. Enormous *Planet of the Apes*-type brown monkeys swung from branch to branch. If you venture off on that course, you may never be found again. It's the wild. You're in the jungle, baby.

A month later, Mark helped set up a birthday round for me at Ria Bintan, a Gary Player gem of a track in Bintan, Indonesia. On the ferry with us was my colleague Shane. We landed in Bintan and received the VIP welcome: we breezed through customs, a black SUV whisked us off to the course, and a wonderful hostess nicknamed Chika took care of all our incidentals.

Once we arrived at the clubhouse, we had a fantastic breakfast with John, the managing director of Ria Bintan. He was a good buddy of Mark's and took care of us all day. The vista in that clubhouse is a uniquely gorgeous experience. The view is fully open, overlooking an impossibly beautiful layout of mint green fairways lined with palm trees and views of the South China Sea.

Using Mark's ten-year-old Wilson irons with their worn grips, I did what I could to get the feel and enjoy a round of absolute serenity. I recall the vision of stunning tropical beauty as we were driving the roundabout cart path on the way to the first hole. When you are from North America, being in Asia is a new world. It's literally the opposite side of earth, complete with a different feel from the grass, vegetation, animals, to even the oxygen. And as much as it is unique, the game of golf brings everyone to the same playing field.

The golf course itself was perfect. Just make sure you bring enough balls because you are not finding any wayward drive. Very penal with no real escapes—this is a target golf experience. It's funny that there are guys sitting around the course who sell balls packaged in clear plastic bags. I picked up a dozen Titleist for twenty dollars and lost about half of them. There's a formidable business for you!

On the seventh hole, we pulled up to the tee box and I noticed a carved, gray stone sign with the words "Monkey Crossing" scribed in yellow. As if on cue, a line of monkeys came prancing by like a family on a day trip. We waited for what seemed like ten minutes for the family of gray-bearded, long-tailed macaque monkeys to cross the tee box area. Each of them squawked and walked with a sprite step. Some even looked back at us with smiles as if to welcome us to Bintan—or to taunt us. I'm not sure which.

It changed my entire day to witness the utterly natural joy those creatures had as they walked by us, hand in tail with the next one in line. The words that immediately popped into my mind were *blissful simplicity*. I imagined seeing those words written in beautiful flowers, spelled out for me in the middle of the fairway. If you can live wildly in Indonesia in a breathtakingly manicured piece of real estate, surrounded by crystal blue waters, an abundance of food, and freedom, wouldn't you be full of joy?

My goal after that serene scene was to make "blissful simplicity" the theme of the round. Not playing with my own clubs, ten-thousand miles from home, I was on a track that swallowed golf balls like Cookie Monster swallows chocolate chips. Keeping it simple and blissful was the name of the game.

When you're in a place so gorgeous on foreign soil, it is really easy to slip into a kind of meditative place of thankfulness for your surroundings, grateful for the opportunity to play in Indonesia as a birthday present. Throughout the day, Mark, John, Shane and I laughed and told stories.

Mark and John were from Singapore, Shane was an Aussie, and then there was me, an American. The chatter is a bit more interesting when it's with people from completely different worlds. We traded tales, jokes, and talked smack to each other all day. Trash talk has no language barrier. There may have even been a few small wagers. We were from everywhere, and golf made our improbable meeting possible.

When remembering my round at Ria Bintan, I think of my two best swings.

On the back nine, I found myself in a fairway bunker. All day at this point I was having a blast, but not really playing my best as I was fighting slippery grips and getting used to the feel of those older, clunky clubs. I was about two hundred yards away, so I took out the 5-iron. The bag was so huge, it looked like it only had two clubs in it because of all the room in the club dividers.

I proceeded to step into the bunker, gripping up on the club to give myself a bit more control. I had a clean lie, sizing up my target, I saw my playing partners already near the green, looking back at me. The pressure was on. I put an 80 percent, controlled move on it, with an exaggerated slow backswing. I picked it clean! It came off the club like a rocket, straight at the flag, landing about ten feet from the pin. My second-best shot of the day.

As I got up to the green, Shane said in his charming Aussie accent, "Crackin' shot, mate!" I tipped my cap, marked my ball, and lipped out. What can I say? It wasn't my putter.

My best shot of the day, however, was when I drove it over the green on number twelve. It was a tight dogleg left divided by indigenous trees. I was using John's TaylorMade M3 driver all day and had it dialed in. Crushing my drive over the trees, I was excited to see where it ended up. Riding up to the green, I couldn't find the ball. Maybe it was lost? The chance I took to put on a little show for the boys. After a few minutes, our caddy found it about ten yards long, right off the green, where it lay in tall grass about five feet from a cliff overlooking the sea. I was close to OB but not quite. Got up and down for birdie. A birthday bomb and an up and down for the books, with a majestic background as my witness.

We must have collectively lost two dozen balls that day, but it was the most fun I ever had losing pearls. Some shots weren't even that horrific—the vegetation was just so thick, it left zero room for error. Plus, when you play a new track, you don't really know where your misses will go. It's hit and pray all day.

We had a nice little sandwich at the turn with plenty of Bintan beers and laughs. A hit and giggle loop, for sure. After the round, we took showers, had lunch, and they sang "Happy Birthday" to me with a single candle in a cupcake. A special moment with three new friends. From different corners of the globe, we came together like brothers to play golf on a pristine track. Just a bunch of grown-up kids playing a game. A day of blissful simplicity.

Back at the office the next day, Shane was asked by our colleague who won—meaning between him and me—trying to stir up a little competitive trouble. Shane cleverly replied, "The course won." I laughed and nodded in agreement. It was the truth.

After getting off the lift and walking toward my apartment in Clarke Quay, I got to thinking: *Actually, I won*—for the opportunity to live and work in Singapore, for Mark who set up a phenomenal round for us to play Ria Bintan, for the new friends, the good shots, and the memories created. That was a victory in and of itself.

Golf is a lot of things: A game, a passion, a walking meditation. But really, it's a chance to experience the world in so many different ways because you must play the earth itself, wherever you are in the world. Every undulation, body of water, grass type, tree, flower, natural hazard, and indigenous animal is in play. It is such a unique sporting experience. The land is your field and you only have two instruments to navigate it: the tools (clubs) you wield and, of course, your mind—the ability to strategize and make certain choices every step of the way. A little like life itself, I suppose.

GAMESMANSHIP

My grandfather was a master at the short game. His grip was like iron, always on point, always hit a straight ball, and he was deadly around the greens. I may have out-driven him by a hundred yards, but he'd get up and down from anywhere and make that twelve-foot putt for par nine out of ten times. He'd let you know it, too. Because he was also a master at trash talking.

When I'd line up to hit a drive, he would look into the woods and tease me, saying, "That's where you're ending up." He was a competitive beast and would use smack talk to get in my head. I didn't know it at the time, but this was straight-up gamesmanship, which is essentially mind games using various ploys and tactics to gain a psychological advantage. When I was younger and new to the game, the ploys worked. I'd blow a drive into the woods, and my grandfather would give me his "I told you so" laugh.

It's not that he wanted me to play badly—but he *did* want to beat me. And he was from the old school, so hitting a long ball with my Big Tech driver was not important or impressive to him. He'd rather see me hit a 3-iron in the fairway than have to chop out of the woods. And to be honest, he wasn't wrong. But I was determined to get my drive under control and hit a bomb in the fairway—and would practice my game until I was consistent.

What his smack talking gamesmanship taught me, though, is how to play under a little pressure. Now when a fellow player chatters to get in my head or razzes me about a bad shot, it doesn't bother me as much—not after dealing with my grandfather when I was a kid. Instead, it's become fuel for my competitive spirit. I began using it as a sort of reverse psychology: *I want you to talk smack. I want to shut you the eff up. Go ahead, it's only going to motivate me more.*

No one on earth did this better or with more absolute tenacity than Michael Jordan. This well-known fact was driven home in the ESPN miniseries *The Last Dance.* From Magic Johnson to Karl Malone to Gary Payton, and especially Isiah Thomas, Jordan would look for literally *anything* to get pissed off about because it would motivate him. Anything you say or do can be used against you in the court of Jordan. And I believe a lot of the greats do this. Think about the daily grind of being a pro athlete. How do you get up for *every single game* all the time? You need that extra push to accelerate you to always be better, to compete at the highest level, day in, day out.

As I got better at the game, older, and stronger, my grandfather would still pull those tricks out of his bag. I would laugh and pipe it down the middle and tell him, "Long doesn't always mean out-of-bounds!" Then I'd go and duff a chip, and he'd get on me about that. "I told ya, s(h)ee?" He talked like those sports commentators in the old movie reels from the 1930s, during the Babe Ruth era.

To put all the aspects of your game together is the constant challenge and ever-present beauty of golf. Knowing you put in your practice time with both your swing game *and* mental game adds a little confidence, making it easier to block out any outside interference or annoyance.

As long as you play this game, there will always be something you can improve—and there will always be another bad shot or circumstance where a level of trash talking is in order. But do it at your own peril. The Golf Gods are always listening. What goes around, swings around.

NOT THROWIN' AWAY MY SHOT

What kind of player are you?

In the Broadway musical *Hamilton*, Alexander Hamilton's main number is about not throwing away his chance to make history. He is an ambitious immigrant from the West Indies, fully understanding that without the American Revolution, he will never make his mark on the world. For him, the alternative is anonymity. He is not going to waste this once-in-a-generation shot.

But for you, throwing away your shot means trying to do too much.

Say you are a 20+ handicap, you nutted your drive on a par 5 and now have 250 yards to the green. As you stare down at your 3-wood in the bag, remember you have a choice. You can lay up with a 7-iron, play a wedge in for a good birdie chance, or you can hit the best 3-wood of the year—because you know that's what it will take—and play for the miracle.

Your best bet may be to go with the higher percentage play of laying up with a more controllable club, hitting what is more familiar to you.

An important factor in laying up is being aware of how many yards to the pin you will leave yourself. Play toward your strengths. If you are a solid wedge player, hit the club that will leave you that wedge yardage into the green. Do the calculation in your head from where you lie, then execute a good swing with the right club that will leave you that distance. There is no question this will allow you more opportunities to make birdies (and pars).

Is it more conservative? Yes. Is it smarter? Hell yes. Don't throw away your shot if you want to score better.

The frustration of pulling your fairway wood and topping it into the woods or slicing it out of bounds is not worth it. If you are tempted to go for it, and you think to yourself, "We didn't get all dressed up for nothin'!" like William Wallace in *Braveheart* (insert Scottish accent), then by all means, rise up and go for it. If you pull it off, fantastic. If you do not, learn from it—and then reread this chapter.

When you look back on history, the dramatic irony is that Alexander Hamilton *did* throw away his shot in his duel with Aaron Burr. As a result, he tragically lost his life at forty-seven years old. In your case, the only thing you will lose is a stroke or two.

And let's keep it real-a-second (for just a millisecond)—your golf round is unlikely to be made into a Broadway musical.

So, when you are faced with the challenge of a particular shot, and you are calculating the risk/reward factor, just think of *Hamilton*, and sing to yourself, "I'm not throwin' away my shot . . ." You may not need to risk your life for your country, but why risk a stroke?

Play within yourself. Go with your strengths. Your scorecard will thank you.

QUICK WARM-UP

You show up to the course late for your tee time because you slept in, or you opted for Starbucks instead of giving yourself the time to hit balls at the range. For any amateur golfer, life often gets in the way of preparation time. You figure when you aren't that great to begin with, what difference will hitting a few extra range balls make? Besides, you are craving that blonde roast oat milk latte. You convince yourself that you need coffee more than you need to know the speed of the greens.

Not to fear, though! With some structured efficiency, you can still give yourself a proper warmup. If you don't have much time before a round, carve out a few minutes where you can warm up your body and the key aspects of your game. The main goal of this preparation is to get yourself ready to play mentally and physically. You want to enjoy yourself—and not pull your back out on the third hole. The idea is to get your heart rate going, get the blood flowing, and ready your body to play golf.

Think of a boxer before they enter the ring. They always have beads of sweat on their forehead, glistening in the arena lights as they walk down the aisle bumping to some hip-hop tune. Their trainer just worked their asses hard in the dressing room to get them warm. You cannot go into a fight cold. If you do, your reflexes will not be as sharp, you will lack speed and power. It is a recipe for disaster and quite possibly, a KO. If you ever see a fighter go into a ring dry, put money on the other guy.

The same rules apply to your golf game.

Take the five to ten minutes to do what you can to gain the confidence you're warmed up enough to play decently—and to know you won't pull anything or hurt yourself.

Like your pre-shot routine, it's essential to develop a warmup routine you can go to any time you play. Even a PGA Tour pro like Jordan Spieth has a regular routine that is a half-hour long and a shorter fifteen-minute version. As an amateur, it may still take you six holes to be playing with a certain level of comfort, but remember, this game is mental. Even the slightest bit of warmup and stretch preparation can make the difference between feeling ready to play or being tight and unsure.

Here are ways you can warm up when you have a short amount of time before your tee off:

YOUR BODY

WARMUP

First and foremost, you want to get the blood pumping. If you start by stretching cold muscles, it could result in pulling or straining them. Obviously, this would have an adverse effect, like hurting yourself and playing even worse than you would have. For starters, warm up in the car. You can stretch your back and loosen your wrists and ankles as you drive to the course.

When you get to the playing field, the simplest of warmups will do. Walk around the parking lot for a few minutes. Throw in some lunges and jumping jacks if you want to get the heart pumping a bit faster.

STRETCHING

Now you're breathing a bit heavier and your blood is pumping, you're ready for some basic stretching. Knowing that you have only a few minutes, make sure you are focusing on the body parts that work the hardest when you swing a club.

Dynamic stretching is extremely effective, along with active movements where joints and muscles go through a full range of motion. The golf swing uses seventeen different muscle groups. When you stretch, make sure you are hitting three key areas of your body: your back, hip flexors, and your chest.

There are an infinite number of ways to loosen up these body parts. No special tools are needed. You can grab a couple of clubs and go through an entire routine. Trust that when you put some time into loosening up, your chance of injury will go *down* and your percentages of playing better will go *up*.

Check out videos of four-time European Ryder Cup team member, Miguel Ángel Jiménez. That guy has been on tour for forty years and has a record of over 700 starts on the European Tour. He's legendary for his hardcore warmups for good reason—it increases longevity and helps avoid injury.

Now it is time to take some rhythmic practice swings and walk over to the chipping area—if you have time.

CHIPPING

When you can't get a full range sesh in, chipping can be just as effective as hitting balls with full swings because you are practicing hitting the ball through the *impact zone*. You are getting a feel of the ball meeting the face of the club.

Not only that, but you are also getting your tempo down. If you can make a few nice chips, bump and runs, flop shots, medium-distance pitches, and there is consistency with them all, then you are dialing in your tempo. Watch it translate to the rest of your bag during your round.

To quote legendary teacher Harvey Penick:

"To warm up in a hurry and arouse your sense of feel, use the time you have to stroke a few careful pitch shots. This will put your mind on the business at hand—which is to play golf."[2]

PUTTING

Loren Roberts was one of the best putters on the PGA Tour. In his quick warmup advice, he spoke of one-handed putting to get the speed of the greens. If you are rushed to get out to the first tee, take three balls out and hit a few long putts one-handed. Note how the greens are rolling. Feel your right hand meet the ball—or left if you are left-handed.

Then practice one-handed three to five-footers. Watch the ball fall in the cup. It's a confidence booster to see putts going into the hole right before you go to the first tee, especially when you're only using one hand.

Arnold Palmer said if you've only got a few minutes before you tee off, practice thirty-footers, and finish with downhill left-to-right putts. I tend to listen to the King anytime I hear his advice.

Doing one of these two exercises—or a combination—for a few minutes will surely give you a feel for the greens you are about to play. It will also help you become more confident with your stroke on the first green.

YOUR MIND

VISUALIZING

Before you tee up your first ball, put that new Pro V back in your bag and pull out the Pinnacle. Just kidding.

Actually, if you're feeling it, have the balls to tee up the new pearl. The key here is to use the time to set some goals for the day before you even drive that tee into the turf. Picture your swing being fluid. Confidently know your body is ready to perform for you.

If you did not have time to do any of the above club work or stretching, at least look over the scorecard and mentally prepare for the holes you are about to play. Strategize how you will approach the first few. Because visualization is so incredibly powerful, it will lead you to do exactly what you've programmed into your brain.

Close your eyes and visualize playing your best. Take three deep breaths, open your eyes, and zero in on your first target.

Now forget everything and enjoy your round.

CROSS-COUNTRY GOLF

WARNING:

Only play when there is no one on the course.

For (semi)professionals only.

Do not try this at home.

Cross-Country Golf is a game where you redesign the golf course you are playing *while* you are playing. My warning above isn't a joke. This is only recommended when there are not many other players around *and* if you have the skills to pull it off. Both criteria are of the utmost importance. If you have one without the other, do *not* play this game!

The challenge: If you are playing a somewhat empty course, and you are standing on the tee box on number 13, and you can reach the number 7 green with an iron, why not play a different hole? Tee one up and play a new par 3. If you are on a tee box and can pull the driver out, aim toward an entirely different fairway, hit the shot—maybe make par on that new hole. Combine holes and redesign the track.

You create a whole new golf course on the one you're playing. If you have the time to practice and the course is open, imagine different holes and play them for yourself. Keep things interesting. Have fun and don't hurt anybody. I am not recommending doing this for eighteen. One or two maximum per round is sufficient. Playing the hole out is optional. Just hit the shot.

This is for the daredevil in you. It is for those of you who like to go against the grain, who may have been troublemakers and class clowns in school. It's for those who aren't shy and want to take a shot and mess around when the track is open and you're playing a practice round. This game is about challenging yourself while imagining and executing new shots.

Create new holes on the golf course while you're playing.

This is mostly recommended on your home course or a track you know extremely well. It is *not* recommended if it's the first time you're playing a course and is *especially* frowned upon if the course is crowded. Hurting someone is not cool and *not* the idea here. Having an exhilarating time reimagining the normal shots you usually hit is the idea.

When you can safely play Cross-Country Golf, it's fun as hell.

— SIX —

TRANQUILO

YOUR FLOW

WE'VE ALL FELT THAT FEELING OF BEING "IN THE ZONE" OR "IN THE FLOW"—that ideal moment where mind, body, and soul are in sync perfectly and you perform optimally. It's almost a hypnotic state when things work seamlessly and everything is aligning in a way natural physics can't explain.

Many studies have been done on the minds of top athletes while they perform, proving that certain changes do occur in the brain—including elevated dopamine levels, a feeling of control over your body and surroundings, and self-consciousness disappearing as your awareness intertwines with action. The brain wave frequencies change from high-frequency "beta" waves to lower-frequency "alpha" waves.[1] When these brain waves are being transmitted, you are nowhere in time but the here and now. You are sharp, creative, and your movement is athletic. This is where a player is fully encapsulated in the action at hand, not thinking at all.

Finding your flow very much requires the match between your skills and the level of challenge at hand. If a task is too easy, it can lead to boredom. If it is too difficult, it can bring about frustration and a loss of interest. Getting in the zone is much easier when your interest and skills are balanced. Obviously, finding the flow can be fleeting; it's not necessarily easy to snap your fingers, then automatically shoot your best round. Discovering flow requires surrender, not force; nurture the seed with increased awareness and attention, for flow is like a river—just go with the current.

You can ingrain simple techniques that bring you closer to a place of serenity on the golf course, such as meditation (body, mind, and soul reset), breathing techniques (calming the nervous system), positive self-talk (words create emotions), and visualization (see and believe). Your pre-shot routine can incorporate all of the aforementioned. Taking the time to get comfortable with your mental pre-shot routine, and perhaps even mastering it before you bring it to any competition, will make it easier to use when you need it most. These methods will assist with tension control and help inform your body language. They'll bring you back to the moment, allowing you to stay focused on your target, creating the optimal conditions to help you get in your zone.

Regardless of your circumstances or the pressure you feel in the moment, you can only ask yourself to do your best. That consists of being your own good friend and taking some of the stress out of the situation. Challenges are a constant in life and sports, and once our mind gets in the way, it tends to exaggerate the circumstance or escalate into a psych-out.

It's always good to have a little pressure on—just enough to give you an adrenaline boost motivating you to focus more. Harvey Penick recommends practicing with some competitive structure to realistically "stress test" your skills. When something is on the line, you're that much more interested in the outcome, therefore, much more attentive, committed, and engaged. When you compete in training, it's way easier to perform when it matters.

The essence of you playing your best is really a combination of natural instinct and control. When the two are in harmony, you move closer to achieving your flow. It is all about the balance. If you have natural instinct—your athleticism—set to the extreme, your playing will be more unscientific and lack technical expertise. Yet trying to control your mind too much makes your play become less conscious and overly mechanical. The balance of both aspects is where science meets art—and where you can find your flow.

With practice, you will develop the necessary skills to have a calm, positive, and focused mind more frequently when preparing to hit a golf shot. With repetition, it gets easier to manage your attention, eliminate negative thoughts, and stay connected with your intention as you prepare to swing.

Like every other aspect of your golf game, this is something you must practice until it becomes second nature. Optimizing your performance can become a more common occurrence when you balance your athletic ability with a serene mind.

YOUR INNER iPOD

"He who sings frightens away his ills."
—Miguel de Cervantes

Golf is very much a mental game. And it is of utmost importance to stay clear-headed during a round, or when you practice. Staying open-minded gives you the best opportunity to play well, and playing well equals more enjoyment. It is a very simple equation.

One easy and fun way to achieve your Zen is to think of a song—a Top 40 hit, your favorite, your least favorite, whatever gets that groove going in your soul. Sing it to yourself as you imagine your shot—or shout it aloud if it works for you. Either way you do it, keep the tune going and make your swing. This is an easy trick to keep your mind off mechanics, allowing you to swing more freely. Having a song in your head keeps your mind open and amused—and it also makes your time on the course much more entertaining.

It is highly recommended to try this with your golf partners. You can set the tone of a golf outing with one song. Start to sing it out loud before you tee off and more often than not, your playing partner(s) will finish the lyric with you. This simple mind game increases the fun factor, often creating laughter. It also gets everyone's mind off the pressure of the shot, the bad lie they have, or the 3-putt six they just made on the previous hole.

The reality is, no matter how good or bad you are playing, the game goes on and on 'til the break o' dawn. Keeping things light evokes an essence of non-attachment. When you are unattached to any outcome, a cornucopia of possibilities opens up to you. Surrender to the unknown and you'll be amazed at how your game improves. It's also a pleasure to add a little bit of humor and lightness to your golf round. Your playing partners will appreciate the gesture.

For example, any time I hit a bad drive, and watch it sail into the woods, I will often belt out Player's "Baby Come Back." You want that baby to come back, but you're going to be hitting three…either way you sliced it. Might as well make light of it, not carry the agony of a drive that you just effed up. A soundtrack is completely apropos for the situation at hand—it adds more pleasure to the entire experience. And most importantly, it makes your lost stroke less significant.

Having fun equals swinging well.

Songs with duos are especially enjoyable to sing. Get your partner to chime in on the hook when you sing "Livin' on a Prayer." Maybe you are in more of a Queen and David Bowie mood because you're "Under Pressure." Or step up to your ball with a little "Rapper's Delight"—to the rhythm of the boogie, the beat—in your head. Your percentage of hitting the shot you imagine will rise exponentially. Why? Because you're not thinking about it. You've evaluated your lie and distance, envisioned your ball flight, and selected your club—now let the rhythm move you to put a good swing on the ball.

Having fun equals swinging well. Sing your song, play your game, enjoy your time. The practice you put in on the range is much more effective when you're singing your song. There is a tune for every shot in the book. Use music to soothe your soul and filter out any negative emotions like nervousness, stress, or even anger.

To think about music and not your swing, get a good inner beat going. It helps your tempo and serves as a constructive relaxation technique. The beauty is you can do this anytime, anywhere—from your backyard to the driving range to your club championship.

My go-tos are usually a combination of classic rock, 80s hits, hair rock, R&B, or hip-hop. If one of your buddies thinks of that rare song that you haven't heard in a while and belts it out, creating a group sing-along with some belly laughs, well, that's the sweet spot and a certain conversation starter later at dinner.

Sing with passion, swing with ease.

"When we listen to music we are not listening to the past, we are not listening to the future, we are listening to the expanded present."[2]

—Alan Watts

NICE AND EASY

My grandfather was an avid golfer. Obsessed with the game, he was always hitting balls against a huge net in his backyard. He had a garage full of clubs and a workstation where he was always tweaking a putter or adding a new grip to his driver. Golf was a way of life for him. I cannot remember a Christmas where I didn't get him a dozen balls. My grandparents' Christmas tree always had those little Santa ornaments made out of golf balls—a white ball wearing a little red hat and rosy cheeks.

A true man's man, he owned every tool in the book. He eventually got into politics and was a very successful councilman in the town of Sayreville, New Jersey. He actually lived at 3 Rota Drive. Not many people can say they lived on a street named in their honor. He was one-of-a-kind—they don't make them like they used to.

The thing about my grandfather was he'd go all-in on teaching you off the course. *On* the course, the lessons lessened, especially when I was good enough to give him a run. My dad and I used to tease him when the tips ended and the lessons stopped—that moment in the match where it was getting close. He was always a competitor. Grampa would laugh while he hit his shot, knowing we called him out.

Whenever I hit against his net in the backyard, he would say, "Nice and easy..." as I took the club back and forth with multiple practice swings. I can hear his voice to this day telling me to be deliberate in my motion. He taught me the value of slowing down the swing, finding tempo, and being mindful about what

I was looking to do with the ball. "*Niiiice* and easy . . . that's it!" It was such excellent feedback as a young boy to hear him beam proudly at the progress I was making with my swing. He was proud of the quick-study grandkid, and in a way, he was taking credit as well. Justly so.

He had me ask the questions before I hit: Am I hitting it low or high? Left to right or right to left? Am I hitting a full shot or taking a little off of it? Most average players just want to get the ball in the air, flying toward the target. If that is the case with you, a useful key is a thoughtful, deliberate approach to how you swing and where you want to go with the ball.

Stand behind your ball before you swing. Use your pre-shot routine to look at your target and visualize the type of shot you want to hit. Rehearse it with some practice swings while imagining the ball going where you envision it. There is no shot clock in golf. Take the time you need. This will raise the percentages of you hitting the ball where you are aiming because you are visualizing what you want to do.

If you see it in your mind first, the chances are 100 percent better that you can create it in your reality. So many people hit the ball and pray without any pre-shot routine or premeditated thought. Add this nuance to your game and I guarantee you shave three to five strokes a round.

Some prayers do get answered, but to expect the good Lord to make that twelve-footer for you is wishful thinking. I hear His short game isn't His strength, anyway. And the truth is, God helps those who help themselves. This means . . . putting the time in and practicing!

When you feel comfortable over the ball, your target is clear and your alignment feels right, you can pull the trigger with confidence knowing you did all the preparation.

That is when you can swing with confidence and have more access to *your* "nice and easy." Nice and easy is a rule of thumb with any amateur, just the same as taking more club. Take more club and swing nice and easy.

LIVE, GOLF, AND EAT

You're finally on the course and beyond stoked. You thought about it all week, rounded everyone up and now you're on the first tee. Fresh air, beers cracking, you're amped up, adrenaline on high, champing at the bit to take hacks and crush a drive down the fairway. The competitive fire is rising in your stomach.

In the heat of battle, however, it's very common to neglect your basic needs, starting with your body. With all the freedom and excitement, you can be too wrapped up in the game to discern that you need to fuel yourself and hydrate. You cannot concentrate and perform your best when hungry or dehydrated. Daily tasks are difficult when you're lightheaded, much less anything athletic. It's super-important to maintain good hydration levels and drink sufficient fluid. Dehydration can impair your ability to focus, which can lead to fatigue and possibly a loss of skill.

This is important to remember every time you play, especially when it's brutally hot or when you are drinking alcohol. You want to enjoy your drink of choice, but also be aware of your body and what it needs to stay sustained while you swing a golf club for five hours. Your body is your temple, and when you take care of it, it takes care of you.

Golf is a unique game of skill and concentration to be maintained over several hours where the action takes place in small intervals of time. It requires an abundance of skill as well as intense patience and focus. You have to wait your turn, *then deliver* when the time comes to hit your shot.

Your nutrition has an impact on how you perform. A sign of low blood sugar is when you have a hard time focusing or you keep making the same mistake. You may feel a bit more anxiety than usual, maybe even light-headed or fatigued. Those are moments you need to step away from the game and nourish yourself.

It is extremely important to maintain steady blood sugar. You know the old saying, "An apple a day keeps the doctor away." I'll even add that an apple a day can keep your slice away.

When you ignore your body, your game pays the price. Much of the time, a banana and a drink with electrolytes are the magic cure for that little hook or bugaboo you have that day. You forget to take care of yourself, then wonder why your drives aren't going straight or you keep missing putts. Your brain *and* body need to be fed.

Use a mindful approach to nutrition. A snack every four to six holes can be helpful for keeping energy levels up and assisting you in maintaining concentration. Some healthy snacks can include fresh fruit and veggies, dried fruit, pretzels, trail mix, popcorn, beef jerky, granola, and protein bars. You can even make smoothies or use your home juicer to prepare some extra nutrition for the course.

Pause and chill for five to ten minutes, ideally between holes. Take that time off to enjoy sustenance and absorb your surroundings before you get back to the game. Drive the cart to a cool spot on the course with a view, find some shade, and park. Have that half a sandwich and a drink. Take a deep breath.

Experience your five senses. See the beauty around you. Listen to the wind rustle through the trees and leaves. Smell the flowers. Taste your food and drink. Feel the grip of the club in your hands as you take practice swings. Imagine a perfect next shot.

Take a moment to nourish your mind, body, and soul. Be aware of your surroundings. Have gratitude for the moment as it is impossible to have gratitude without being happy.

Enjoy playing healthy golf.

PLAY IN YOUR SLEEP

> "Assume you are that which you wish to be; walk as though you were it; and as you remain faithful to your assumption—it will harden into fact."[3]
>
> —Neville Goddard

Neville Goddard was a profoundly influential mystic. After a career as a Broadway dancer, he became a speaker who authored many books on the law of attraction and how to live with your wishes fulfilled. He educated people about mental processes and the ability to change our situation through *feeling*. He taught how we are co-creators in partnership with universal law, and by using imagination with emotion, we have the ability to bring about our desires.

Some of his ideas were influenced by the nineteenth-century French psychologist Émile Coué, who was a pioneer in the use of self-hypnosis. He maintained that through conscious autosuggestion such as mantras, we can change our unconscious thought, which then reflects in the outside world. He believed we can make lasting changes in our lives through using imagination.

In his law of assumption, Neville brilliantly conveyed how to attract results through a simple technique of assuming anything you desire solely through imagination and mental fortitude. In other words, think from the *end*. When you *assume and feel* where you want to be—possess what you would like to attain or are shooting the score you seek—then life has a way of meeting your assumption.

One of his most effective teachings to attract what you wish for is to imagine it while you drift off to sleep. The powerful instances before you pass out are like heightened meditative moments where you can directly access your subconscious mind. It is to think from the end with passionate desire. It is to know what the result looks like and let your subconscious fill in the blanks along the way to get you to that result.

Neville places a ton of emphasis on the importance of falling asleep with the feeling of your desire fulfilled. The desire needs to be straightforward and filled with joy and excitement. No half-assing what you look to achieve. He maintained that our mental creativity is greatly enhanced when we enter this state of *hypnagogia*. The hypnagogic state is that relaxed moment in between—that half-drowsy, half-awake time before you pass out.

To be effective here requires a bit of conscious control over what you see in your mind's eye. Be deliberate. Remember, when you are picturing your fulfilled goal, the essential key is to experience the *emotions* you will feel when you achieve your aim. If you want to break 90 (or 80 or 70), *feel* it. If you want to win against your friend, picture your score lower than theirs on the card and experience the emotion of satisfaction.

As your subconscious is the master during sleep, it takes that *feeling* and manifests what you will experience in your consciousness while you are awake. Try it for yourself. The night before you play and are drifting off to sleep, imagine the round you want to have, and the actual feeling of satisfaction and pride after playing the best golf of your life.

Sense how you would hit a perfect shot. Acutely imagine the feeling in your hands of the ball compressing off the clubface. Visualize a beautiful ball flight from your POV: the ball in the air as you hit your drive. Get as detailed as possible. Visualize the golf course, what you are wearing, the smell of the grass and flowers, and how limber your body feels.

Embody the feeling of the flow, when everything is in sync and you are playing the round of your life. Don't picture yourself as if looking at a screen, do it as if you are there yourself—reality from *your* point of view. Your own personal *Truman Show*, except at the end, you play better golf.

If imagination is not your strength, then simply envision yourself signing a low score on your scorecard. Picture your friends high-fiving you. Visualize smiling in the bar afterward and being congratulated. Affirm it to yourself as being real right now at this moment.

Remember always: thoughts become things. And how fun is it to just imagine holing out for an eagle from 125 out? Or crushing a 300-yard drive down the fairway, driving up to it in the cart thirty yards ahead of all your friends? Put that reel in your mind of draining putt after putt. The more specific you can visualize, the better. Your subconscious does not know the difference between imagination and reality, so see it and emotionally rise to the occasion.

Emotionally rise to the occasion.

If you know the course you'll be playing, you can get a distinct picture in your mind of each hole. You can imagine the iron you'll hit on that par 3 or how you'll approach that challenging par 5 on the back nine. Play the course before you play the course. Use your creativity to improve your game before even lacing up your golf shoes.

Use your creativity to improve your game.

Become a pro in your mind. Then watch it become your reality when you play. Recognize that an unwavering self-belief is the key to unlocking your success. Your subconscious mind holds the blueprint for your future, shaping your destiny in ways you might not even realize. But this blueprint isn't set in stone. With focused intention, you can reshape your destiny and sculpt the future you desire. It just takes practice and self-discipline to maintain the attitude of the wish-fulfilled.

The equation is as follows:

1. Define your desire clearly and without hesitation.

2. Quiet your mind and enter a state of deep relaxation, verging on sleep.

3. Visualize the assumption while embracing the sensation of the fulfilled wish.

Immerse yourself in this mental motion picture, play it over and over again until you actually *can* feel a sense of fulfillment. Let your imagination run free. Feel "as if" with absolute conviction, and you are bound to encounter your desire. This ingrained belief is more powerful than just wishing—it's rewiring your perception of reality. There is a huge difference between feeling something and merely knowing it intellectually. This is beyond faith—it is the powerful perception of reality as *already* being the way you envision.

You don't always need a club and ball to practice. Sometimes you can go to the range in your mind. Drift off to sleep thinking about those five-foot putts dropping or that chip shot landing a foot from the pin. Fall asleep happy and grateful. Let your subconscious rule and allow it to work for you while you sleep. Assume and feel it.

Assumption is true co-creation. The future becomes the present when you already are what you will be.

STRESSOR COOKER

It's a different type of golf when there is pressure and competition. It's a new game when you play for more than your own score, when there is money on the line, when you have a teammate relying on you, or both. It's challenging enough to hit a good golf shot in a fun round on a weekend, but to hit it when bragging rights hang in the balance is a different story altogether. It gives you a very small, if not microscopic clue of what the pros feel every week. This can either disrupt your performance or be a stimulant to thriving. It all depends on the way you cope with the situation at hand.

Pressure manifests itself mentally, physically, and emotionally. When you are under duress, your heart rate speeds up and your breath becomes shallow—it can feel like you're hyperventilating. The ability to think clearly becomes harder, you may forget how to do the simplest things, such as forgetting your grip by holding on so tightly you lose your feel. Your mental sharpness may decline, disrupting your capacity to execute at your best. Pressure has a huge impact on your ability to make correct decisions. You are in a state of panic and rush, often resulting in the opposite of what you intend.

Just think of a quarterback being hurried and throwing an ill-advised interception. Their timing is disrupted, decision-making is forced, and they do not have the time to think clearly. The results are usually horrible as everything seems like it is in disarray. Sometimes these decisions are the difference between winning and losing.

The sporting event contains no pressure in and of itself. This is important. There is zero pressure in the event itself. Pressure is a block created by the athlete. How you view this stressful moment will determine your internal response. Do you see the situation as a challenge or threat? Your perception will dictate how you perform.

Ignoring the pressure only makes it worse. This is when you need to take it head-on and use the mindfulness skills you have acquired to be flexible and persevere.

1. **Relish in the Moment**

It's so fun to play golf with something riding on it. Pressure can be your friend. Use it as an opportunity to test your skills. See for yourself how all your practice has paid off. And talk some smack once you do. Go out and win the match.

2. **Don't Give a F@%k**

Make it insignificant. Let go of the outcome. The more important the result is (or seems to be), the more stress you will feel. If you know you've done the preparation and have spent sufficient time in the dirt, the less anxious you will feel. Appreciate being in nature. Just surrender to the moment and do your best. Remember, you'll either win or you will learn.

3. **Breathe**

The character Danny Rojas from the hit show *Ted Lasso* always states, "Football is life." But the truth is, *breath is life*. Focus on the process. Make sure you are breathing, filling your lungs with oxygen. Tell yourself to "chill" as you exhale. This is the most basic and effective technique you can use to destress. It will bring you a sense of calm and keep you in the now. Deep breaths are like magical reset buttons for your nervous system.

4. **Focus on What You Can Control**

The single most important practice in Stoic philosophy is differentiating between what you have influence over and what you do not. The only thing you *can* control is your thoughts, attitude, and how you swing the club. As soon as you hit that ball, you have zero control over what happens next. The only thing you can control is your reaction to the end result of the shot and/or the outcome of the match itself. Jack Nicklaus was just as gracious in defeat as he was in victory. A true gentleman. Be like Jack.

5. **Positive Thoughts, Positive Vision**

It is very easy to slip into negative inner dialogue when you're in a pressure situation or behind in a match. Remember, your inner self-talk is everything. How you speak to yourself will dictate what your brain will hear, and the actualized result will follow. Thinking of a positive outcome increases your resilience. Keep it simple, see your next shot going exactly where you are aiming. Any happy thought in your mind will do. Positive thought begets a more positive attitude and vision. Catch yourself when you are slipping down the negativity slope. Replace any bad thought with a good one.

The overall sentiment of this list is simply: *never let 'em see you sweat.* In any competitive match, your opponent will seize any sign of weakness. Pay attention!

Body language will say more about them or you than you will realize at the time. Your sweaty palms, constant fidgeting, and avoiding eye contact will not go unnoticed by a seasoned competitor. Effective leaders and successful athletes are experts at keeping their cool and appearing unfazed. At the very least, they are experts at *acting* that way.

In competition, any edge you can gain makes the difference

between victory and defeat. That is why the psychological aspect of golf is of paramount importance. As Sun Tzu says in *The Art of War*:

"Be extremely subtle, even to the point of formlessness. Be extremely mysterious, even to the point of soundlessness. Thereby you can be the director of the opponent's fate."

No athlete can escape the stressor cooker. It is all about reframing the situation and using simplicity as your ally—breathe, visualize, and go back to the basics. When emotions run high, we have to rely on these simple actions to bring us back to center.

Think of this time as a golden opportunity to show yourself what you can do. Pressure is a privilege. Pretend you're Tiger on the back nine at The Masters or Tom Brady in the Super Bowl. The key for you is to find the sweet spot where the stressor cooker triggers your engaged, zoned-in mindset to help you thrive at crunch time.

Make pressure your b*tch.

— SEVEN —

HOME FIELD ADVANTAGE

THERE IS NO SPOON

YOU SWING YOUR SWING, THE BALL GOES WHERE IT GOES. You project your soul (the ball) into the universe. You can only control so much—your part. The wind, the trees, the lie, the type of grass—these elements are all out of your control. Like life, you have to play it where it lies. You must pass through the threshold of regret, anger, and frustration, and let go of the past to be in the present.

You are not your thoughts. The voice in your head is not even you. You're not even your physical form. All you see is a hologram that exists purely through your own consciousness. There is no spoon and the only thing that exists is right now!

Being conscious and in the present is the best way to achieve optimum results. And as consciousness is the only reality, what you think or believe is the truth—to you.

Leave your last stroke in the past. It doesn't exist any longer. Depriving it of attention will make it fade away. It doesn't matter if it didn't go well. That doesn't mean you cannot hit it pure this time. You've been given another chance.

Remember, the world you observe moment to moment is much like a screenshot of your mind. Even if you do not think you have the skills to pull off a challenging shot, imagine you can anyway. Clear your head, focus, and make a slow, smooth swing. You only have NOW. Which is to say, you only have this next shot.

Be mindful about it and make it count. As long as you're breathing, you will always have another stroke to play. If it doesn't work out, well, you have another shot to make it up. And another shot after that.

THE MAGIC CARPET

The owner of the carpet shop poured more tea into my glass cup—a taste bud blast of perfect mint. We walked barefoot on a hundred square yards of Moroccan rugs sprawled beneath our feet as we sipped the tea, strolling upon a living history of culture and artistry. As we did, he went on about the history of Berber carpets—which began around the seventh century—all hand-woven, just like the ones we were standing on. An ancient technique, unchanged over centuries. As I stepped on rug after rug, the feeling of Moroccan tradition and heritage rose from my soles *to* my soul. The feeling of cultural appreciation still resonates deeply.

The shop at the Jemaa el-Fnaa market in Marrakesh is a kind of speakeasy, found in the maze of the medina. Behind its exquisitely carved doors, it is like a museum with bright lights, shiny white marble floors, colossal crystal chandeliers hanging from fifty-foot-high wood ceilings, and wall-to-wall carpets.

To see another, I pointed, and a bunch of hands took it down and rolled it out in a matter of seconds. These carpets are made of pure wool and are intricately designed with unique patterns and colorful symbols—the vibrant dyes and impeccable workmanship are something to behold. Each one is uniquely handcrafted and takes years to complete. The knot patterns differ on each rug—some dig in like fingers giving a foot massage while others are soft and fluffy as if walking on a cloud.

After a customary haggle, I chose a remarkably stunning Beni Ourain carpet. It is one of the plushest, fuzzy soft rugs you'll ever walk on, the epitome of luxury and opulence. Undyed, made with 100 percent sheep wool, its unique patterning is made with the most refined Berber artistry. The carpet was sent to the US, and as the rug was being unrolled, it instantly filled my place with a Moroccan essence, exuding a Berber, African, Arab, and Jewish influence. Standing on the magic carpet is like teleporting directly back to Marrakesh. The vibe is real.

My place has twenty-foot ceilings and long hallways, which makes it a great indoor Wiffle ball range. I hit wedges, irons,

even the occasional wood—and can track the first twenty yards of ball flight before it inevitably hits off the ceiling or walls. Of course, I had to slap a golf ball off the rug, just to see how it felt.

To my utter amazement, the sheep wool is the most glorious surface to not only stand on (barefoot), but to swing on, and it simulates grass perfectly. Even the scaly-shaped patterning helps me line up my club square. I beat the hell out of this rug with my irons, really go after the ball with full swings, flops, pitches, and choke-up punches—the carpet is unfazed. The feeling of fine wool on my feet sends a signal to my brain, baking in the right rhythm-dance-swing-tempo. A proper weight shift from the inside to the outside of the feet, finishing with balance, looking at the target—a particularly useful drill with short irons and wedges.

It's fascinating how when a ball is purely struck, it will pinball around, then return to the *exact* spot I hit it on the rug, oftentimes right up against the blade of my wedge, as if by magnetic force. It's a weird phenomenon that surely can be explained through the physics of ball speed, angles, and distances. But it's more than science—it's a mystical message letting me know I'm doing something right.

For other swings, it's a hit and search mission, and any found ball is a small victory. You don't have to look for good shots.

The plush magic carpet is a luxurious piece of fine art that is decorative, impressive, and a pleasure to the senses. It is a statement piece for your home. It's also a yoga mat, a dance floor—a perfect artificial surface to smack golf balls indoors. And every once in a while, I fly it around the neighborhood.

Find that area of your home that is ideal to practice, especially for those of you who must endure winter weather. Use the space to simulate your game all year long. Chip and putt in an area where you won't bash your TV or break anything of value.

Swinging barefoot on the magic carpet, I can still hear that Moroccan-accented explanation about the detailed history of the rug. And I'd like to think I am adding a bit of unique history to it myself every time I thwack golf balls off the fine wool and watch them rattle around my house.

OLD GUY TO YOUNG SELF

Practicing on a simulator is a fantastic way for the average player to get a look at their numbers. The pros all use the swing trackers on the range. If you watch guys like Max Homa or Scottie Scheffler practice—along with every other player on tour—they are always hitting balls on the range, then immediately checking their ball speed, spin rate, launch angle and, of course, distance.

There is a myriad of data to ascertain when you look at a yardage tracker with every club and shot. And unless you are a serious player, you likely do not have a SkyTrak Launch Monitor readily available for each range session. So whenever you can use a simulator at your local PGA Superstore or even a luxury building, do it. Not just for fun, but to practice and get an idea of *your* numbers.

If you are new to the game, getting a beat on how long you hit each club is invaluable information. Yes, those distances will change as your swing gets more dialed-in, as your club head speed gets quicker, but getting a good idea of your starting point is crucial to improving your game. How else could you know if you are increasing your distance and improving your ball striking? Knowing your distances is imperative if you are serious about getting better at the game of golf.

The statistics the machine tracks give important data which can help you understand more acutely what your tendencies are. As I used my building simulator, hitting a bucket of balls with the house King Cobra irons, I began to trace and recognize trends in my ball speed, launch angle, impact position on the club, and of course, swing speed. When I started my warmup by hitting balls against the screen, my swing speed would hover around eighty-eight—consistent, good numbers on the rental King Cobra set. As I warmed up further, my speed increased—ninety-two, then to ninety-six—all the way to 101 miles per hour. Obviously, these were not my clubs, so I observed the numbers with a grain of salt.

As I took a water break, watching the Yankees get their thirteen-game winning streak snapped by Oakland on the room TV, I realized that if I were seventy-five years old, I'd advise my today-self to keep my swing speed not quite full and be more deliberate about my game. The 80 percent rule says that if you swing at 80 percent of your full speed, you'll gain more control.

Butch Harmon, one of the best golf teachers of all time, advises swinging at 75 percent. I say 80 percent because it is a nice round number and essentially gets you to the same place. To maintain a better rhythm, make a conscious effort to swing at 80 percent of your maximum speed. In both instances, the teaching remains true: Most golfers will make better contact with the ball by having a more controlled swing. You don't need to swing for the fences every time. A full shoulder turn is essential to generating the power released on the downswing. Remember to finish your swing with balance.

To go at 80 percent is not to swing as hard as you can, but to find a nice tempo allowing you to go up and through rhythmically. One way you can practice finding it is by taking any club and swinging back and forth continuously. With a club in hand and a proper grip, begin by setting up as you would on a normal golf shot, then swing without stopping while feeling the rhythm naturally take shape. You'll *experience* the weight of the club head as an extension of your hands. Eventually, you'll find a sweet tempo in there, feeling as if you can swing all day long. This is not a scientific method but could be a way to find your 80 percent, consistent swing tempo.

With all of this in mind, when I was using the simulator, there was no need for me to swing at 101 miles per hour on every swing. Swinging at 80 percent is ideal for a more consistent round—not to mention, a less sore back. The first twenty shots with my swing speed in the high mid-nineties were a straight, cleanly hit ball which flew very consistently. When my swing speed increased, so did the spin on the ball, resulting in hooks and slices more often. Sure, I flushed a few as I was using a driver and two different fairway woods. The trends in my numbers held true. The stats told me that I had way more spin and the ball was not hitting the clubface in the middle as often.

The entire time I've played golf, I've just naturally hit a long ball—not always straight, however. After years of practice and playing, I realize that it really is just a result of swing speed, flexibility, and impact percentage. The stats do not lie—if you find some consistency when you deliberately slow it down, then let muscle memory take over and find that 80 percent swing that gets you the same numbers time and again. Keep in mind that this does not mean less distance either. In fact, it usually means more.

You really do not need to swing more than 80 percent of your full capacity. The golf swing is a complex, athletic movement. Simplification is your friend. Tempo begins in the back swing. You can also study Hideki Matsuyama's move on the ball as he is unusually deliberate when he takes the club back. The 80 percent effect will help you become more of a shot-maker than a free-swinger, more of a pin-seeker than a hope-and-prayer. Watch the numbers—they likely will remain consistent when you find a consistent tempo.

So whatever your 80 percent is, find it. Adopt a controlled swing that gets each club to a predictable, consistent distance. Use a simulator to practice your distances or get yourself a shot-tracker you can use on your smartphone. There are a ton out there these days that are affordable and easy to use.

They say youth is wasted on the young. They also say to respect your elders. In the case of my seventy-five-year-old self, he would advise having the conscious intention to swing slower. It will not only improve your game but will help in avoiding injury. To over-swing is to be out of control. To be out of control breeds inconsistency which can lead to erratic shots, bad scoring, injury, or worse—a half-dozen lost brand new Pro Vs.

If you want to play better golf, listen to your older self, and swing a smooth 80 percent.

CAST YOUR SPELL

"The 'word' is the desire swimming around in your consciousness—seeking embodiment . . . 'I AM' or the awareness of being is the only reality."[1]

—Neville Goddard

Any time before you play, you can journal and script out how your next round will look and feel. You can write in detail or be more general. But keep it succinct.

When you write and when you speak, you are constantly casting a spell over reality. Anything said after "I am" is the most powerful statement you can ever utter. If you write or say, "I am shooting par tomorrow," you may well have taken your first step in achieving it. Let's be honest, you need to put a lot of time in the dirt to *actually* shoot par, and that may not happen overnight. The point here is to plant positive seeds in your mind garden.

Plant positive seeds in your mind garden.

Even writing something as simple as, "I am going to have a blast," can do wonders for your psyche. You are predicting your future, plotting your destiny. You can write anything you'd like to achieve on the course the next day. You can begin your sentences with the most powerful phrase of all: "I am." Write any positive affirmative statement that puts a high-vibrational thought in your brain.

Keeping it simple is most effective. Overwriting will give your mind too much to ponder, which inevitably could allow doubt to creep in. This will dull the power of the scripting.

Keep it simple, direct, and effective. Journal your goals. Penning them in ink will make them much more tangible. Write down ideas you can draw on for positive mental imagery—visualize to actualize. Write out a powerful statement or affirmation you can say to yourself when you play. Script it out, then close the book.

Our state of mind is like a magnet and the affirming power of scripting is what will form the event in reality. Take notice of how you feel once you affirm all the positive events you want to take place next time you play. The *feeling* is the secret.

After playing, go back and look at what you wrote. See how much of it came true.

They call it "spelling" for a reason. This is a small way to mentally practice the game of golf. It is a mind hack you can use to tap into your subconscious and find that great player who is inside of you already.

SEE AND BE

Life becomes so easy when you *know* things will work out for you.

Everyone creates their reality through imagination and our moods are the key indicator of this imaginal activity. They tell us how we feel and dictate what circumstances in life we manifest from moment to moment. When we are aware of our moods and conscious that our thoughts become things, we can act with intention. That is the magic formula to living with our wishes fulfilled, the essence of the law of attraction.

Life and golf are interconnected. Just as it takes practice to better your swing, your mental time in the dirt will require repetition. Life treats us how we feel. Begin at this moment to practice as Neville calls it, "the art of imagining." Upgrade your mindset—make it a habit to create a positive mental flow.

Whatever the mind dwells upon is amplified. It magnifies and grows until your consciousness reaches a new state. In other words, you get conditioned to the new reality based on the frequency of your thoughts—the positive or the negative. Like attracts like. As the parable goes, feed the good beast.

It all starts with how you feel about yourself. Use your energy on thoughts and feelings which serve you in healthy ways. The more you are aware of your thoughts, the more you can observe them and detach. Realize that they are not you, just as the clouds are not the sky. Be conscious of deliberately directing your thinking and transmute your inner visions into positive manifestations. Know that the universe has your back.

Recite mantras. Simply claim: "I approve of myself. Infinite good comes to me in infinite ways. I deserve it and accept it now."

To attract better, you have to become better. The first step of any kind of improvement starts in your mind, which will then correspond with the desired change in the outside world. Nothing is more important than how you feel. Have a more disciplined conscious control and intentionally go to a feel-good place.

Willfully using your imagination along with physical practice is *the* difference. It makes the distinction between merely making a swing and hitting a golf shot. It is the contrast between living a life filled with purpose or just reacting to what is.

"Whatever state has your attention, holds your life."[2]
—Neville Goddard

YOUTUBE CAN SWING LIKE A PRO

Say you are going to play next Saturday and it's early in the workweek. If you're at the office or have some time at home in the evening, start to mentally prepare for your round.

A fantastic way to keep the positive mental diet alive all through the week is to watch online videos and observe how the pros swing. Consciously take mental note of what they are doing. Then let your subconscious do the rest of the work. Even if you don't realize it at the time you are watching, your inner mind is taking all sorts of notes on the swings you see—the angle, backswing, impact position, balance, and finish.

Observing the swings of the pros is a simple and highly effective way to understand the look and feel of what you need to do yourself. Studies show that learning the golf swing by watching online videos *does* actually help improve your game. Observation aids motor skill learning.[3] The key here is to know that this is not a substitute for physical practice. And to understand what you will get out of watching videos—to get a mental picture of the correct body motion of a swing or putting stroke.

View swings that track the ball with the Toptracer. Notice the ball flight and swing planes. On YouTube, you can view anyone from Ben Hogan to Jack Nicklaus to Lee Trevino to Nick Price to Tiger. Just look them up and absorb the timeless legendary swings of the greatest players of all time. It's like taking a time machine and witnessing the evolution of golf mechanics. They haven't changed all that much.

In addition to watching the greats swing, you can find a video on every aspect of the game online. There is a maze of tutorials—from pros, to coaches, to amateurs alike. But to really simplify the lesson here, it is recommended to watch videos of the finest players making their move on the ball, which will feed your mind with the best kind of mental imagery. There are tons of edits of swings on loop showcasing every player since the camera was invented. You can pause, rewind, and break their swings down in slow motion. It is amazing to watch Hogan swing and compare it to how JT swings today. Study players whose physical stature is comparable to yours.

Watching the pros swing a club is a phenomenal way to bake into your brain the way to move correctly on a ball—everything from proper alignment, to set up, to finish. When you see a professional take a hack at it, you can witness the precision and the tempo. This will no doubt give you a vision of what the right swing looks like—no question about it.

Even watching a PGA Tour event on TV is extremely effective to get a mental picture of the right way to do simple things. That's right, you can even practice this game while sitting on your couch. If you watch closely enough, you will begin to understand the setup and how to address the ball for each kind of shot. These guys play for millions of dollars. This is their livelihood, a day at the office. Observe how they go about their business.

Watch closely the three main phases of the game and how the professionals hit drives, play wedges (one hundred yards and in), and putt.

1. ***Driver:*** They swing freely even when there's a narrow fairway, trouble, or both. They go at it but remain balanced. This is where your 80 percent swing will come in handy.

2. ***Wedges:*** You will notice that all the pros swing without apprehension and finish the shot with their hands, with their hips turning through the ball. It is all about accelerating *through the ball.*

3. ***Putter:*** Tempo, tempo, tempo. Take notice of each of the player's putting stroke and the rhythm in which they take

the putter back and through the ball. Count it out in your head and mimic the rhythm at home.

Scrutinize how the players deal with an errant shot and how amazingly well they always seem to recover. They don't get down about it—they usually use it as motivation to attack even more ferociously. Of course, it is always fun to watch them get pissed off or throw a club—this is hugely cathartic for all amateur golfers and something for us to smile about, for sure. Even the pros are only human, after all. Most of the time they leave that swing in the past, usually playing a beautiful recovery shot that gets the gallery cheering.

The guys on tour can make par from anywhere. And *that* is exactly the mentality you should take away from watching a PGA tournament on television. Allow that to inspire you when going to play your next round. Your inner dialogue will become, "I'll get up and down from anywhere."

It goes without saying that there is no better practice than actually hitting balls. But watching a tour event, taking in how these guys and gals manage the course and deal with each and every shot is a huge lesson for any level player. If you watch closely enough, you can see how their mind works and start to incorporate that into your game. Try to apply the same tempo you are seeing in the videos when you swing your clubs. Do it in front of a mirror and emulate the angles you see, commit the feeling to muscle memory.

Examining how the greats do it helps *you* to become great. This is a constructive way to keep that positive mental diet alive all throughout the week, then take it through your entire next round.

— EIGHT —
LET GOLF

PAR SAVERS

You can picture the scene: Sinking your putt to save par, giving a quick thank-you to your fellow players, grabbing the ball from the cup. You know, *that feeling*. It puts a little glide in your stride and a dip in your hip rolling to the next tee. We've all been there and love it when that ball drops—the relief and optimism as the adrenaline rises in your stomach, especially when you hit a brilliant (or lucky) recovery shot, when par seemed unlikely just five minutes before.

Whether it's a club tournament or a weekend round with your friends at a local muni, par savers are always a huge momentum force. Ideally, you will build off the par putt and use that energy to keep a positive frame of mind. Remaining optimistic is the best way to access your confidence. No matter how your round is going, use the par save as propulsion to keep up the positive self-talk and know whole-heartedly that more good things are coming.

Remaining optimistic is the best way to access your confidence.

You know you are doing this effectively when your next tee shot is well struck and your swing feels natural and flowing, when your putting stroke on the subsequent green feels pure. It's when you feel light and are having a great time just playing.

Never underestimate the power of momentum in all its forms. Momentum is like the tide—it ebbs and flows. Saving par is always a huge momentum push. No harm, no foul, off to the next shot. Missing that putt or taking bogie (or worse) creates a huge difference in your mind and gut walking to the next tee.

Mindset is everything. Be easy on yourself. You do not want to let one or two bad shots ruin your entire round.

There is a negativity bias we inherited as humans which served us a million years ago when we lived in caves, hunted with spears, and ran from saber-toothed tigers. Because of this, our negative events and feelings have more impact on our mental state than positive ones.

Psychologically, the agony of loss is twice as powerful as the fulfillment of gain. Research tells us that negative emotions, like sadness and fear, provoke increased activity in the part of the brain linked to memories.[1] We are wired to dwell on the negative as a matter of survival. You literally have to fight evolution after a bad shot.

Your thoughts and emotions have a great deal to do with your natural rhythm or vibrational frequency. As negative stimuli more strongly influence us, these thoughts trigger a release of hormones affecting your heart rate, often slowing it down or speeding it up to unnatural levels. This will cause a domino effect on your biological state as you will not only ignore the good things around you, but become stuck in a lower vibration because of one single defeatist idea.

The way to recognize you are being self-defeating is to take a moment to check in with yourself. Do you feel frustrated or powerless about your swing or skill level? Is your inner self-talk making you angry? Have you shouted a few profanities? If you believe the shot won't go well, it likely will not. This is a true mind-over-matter moment. Golf is such a test of resolve every single time you swing.

We can shift out of our negativity bias to a more productive mindset by simply noticing when we start getting down on ourselves. Bring awareness to the situation and get yourself back to a better emotional set point. Once you recognize your vibe, you can find a trigger to help bring yourself higher on the happiness scale. It just takes a slight shift in your perception from feeling powerless to empowered. Start with gratitude.

All the more reason to build off your good shots and par savers. Momentum can make or break anything and everything. It is the most delicate wave to ride, and your only intention is to keep riding.

To help maintain your positive flow:

1. Set reachable goals and manage your expectations.

2. Celebrate small victories, such as how many pars you make or good swings you have.

3. Expect challenges and see the opportunity in them.

Rewire your negativity bias into something more optimistic and productive. You *can* and *will* certainly overcome any disappointment you face. But always remember to take the time to grind on those par putts.

Get the result you envision and build momentum. Move on to the next tee with greater expectations. This may be your day.

UNIQUE FOOTPRINT

Your golf swing is your unique footprint.

Your signature, your handwriting. It is the way you laugh, the way you cry. It is your voice.

When you swing the club, no one can swing the club exactly as you do. Yes, technically, it follows the angles and rules of the proper swing, but *the way* you do it—no one does it quite the same way. Or ever will.

The golf swing is your signature in motion. Your tag. Your fingerprint.

Your golf swing is unique to the world. It says something about you that you can't say yourself. A physical message. An athletic telegram from you.

Such a complex athletic motion requires concentration, muscle coordination, balance, and vision.

Your golf swing is your handwriting. Is it hardly legible

scribble—or is it beautiful calligraphy?

Are you loud or soft-spoken? Are you aggressive or timid? Chances are your swing and the way you play reflect exactly those traits you possess in life.

Your golf swing is a reflection of you. It *is* you.

It is the way you dance. The way you sing. Who you are and where you are from. What you do and how you view the world.

More psychics should read golf swings rather than palms. The swing tells you a helluva lot more about a person.

Unspoken and unforced.

A portrait of pure movement painted with every stroke.

TAP THAT

My roommate in Brentwood had a sculpture of a nude woman on all fours, back arched, ass up in the air whipping her hair back as if she was posing for a Playboy pictorial. The piece was about two feet long made of onyx and sat in the center of our mantle above the fireplace. We also had a brand-new Berber carpet and I'd often practice chipping all around our apartment with wiffle balls—and once in a while with real balls, which took balls, so to speak.

When chipping indoors, it helps to have a target—anything to use for a point of focus for proper feedback. To practice flop shots, I often used the sculpture as a point of aim. More specifically, her ass. That onyx booty was pointing straight up in the air begging to be tapped.

The tight lie of the carpet simulated a common chip I had

every weekend. There are myriad links-style courses in LA that are full of tight lies and slippery greens. Friends would sit on the couch and be in hysterics as I called the shot and tapped the ass with the Wiffle ball. The ball would bounce right back to me—like a magic trick.

The game was fun and entertaining for guests, but it had a true purpose. The idea was to really go after the shot with confidence. It was a very tight lie and a delicate chip. With an open wedge, open stance, weight on front foot, head staying down with a purposeful follow-through, I learned to pull off that tricky ten-yard flop shot with more conviction and ease. The rug left no room for error. You really had to be brave and committed. There was no half-assing the off-the-ass shot.

It translated extremely well playing actual rounds because it helped me gain the confidence to go after the ball and finish. My technique became more precise when hitting down on the ball and clipping it just right. It also allowed me to practice controlling the trajectory of the shot. There was a certain arc needed to tap that ass. It was a perfect way to practice at home to gain touch with my wedges—the payoff was obvious when hitting off natural grass.

When amateurs attempt this type of shot, they often fail to have the proper technique and/or ball position, which leads to either sculling it thin or hitting it fat. There's a tendency to scoop the ball in an attempt to "help" it get airborne. First step is ball position. With chipping, you either set up with the ball back in your stance (bump and run), or in the front of your stance (flop). With the flop shot, the idea is to use the bounce of the club, allowing it to slide underneath the ball, popping it up and having it land softly.

The open-faced chip is an absolute necessity if you are looking to lower your score. It also helps improve your putting. The better you get, the shorter your putts will be. You are more likely to make a two-foot putt than a twelve-foot putt. Precisely aim at *where* you want to land the ball, hands in front, clubface open, full finish on your left side. Trust the bounce of the wedge. Imagine how the ball will roll out toward the hole. Feel the pure clip when the clubface passes through the ball. Accelerate fluidly through the finish—get nasty backspin.

The off-the-ass bit had a long, strong run. Tons of laughs, zippy chips, and broken glass. Misses would rattle the mirror above the mantle or break a picture frame. A little damage is worth shaving a few strokes. The price of doing business.

If you look around your home, there are an infinite amount of shots to practice. Think creatively, open your mind to what is possible, and you will start to see things in a different way. The doorknob in the hallway, the over-the-couch flop shot, your kid's Nerf hoop on the door are all contenders. After a while, you will recognize everything as a potential target.

Think creatively, open your mind to what is possible and you will start to see things in a different way.

It is so much more entertaining to add elements of fun to your training time, especially at home. This is a simple way to motivate you to play more frequently, which is the only way to improve your wedge game. It is about repetitive motion, baking that feeling into your conscious awareness.

You never know where your improvement can come from. It could be right in front of you already. Being creative and finding new ways to practice keeps your mind engaged. Who knew that tappin' an onyx booty would shave strokes off my game?

THE ENHANCED EXPERIENCE

The enhanced experience is a vibe. A seasoned player who's been there inherently understands this, even if there is no "enhanced" label specifically slapped on the experience. Everyone wants to play well. An enhanced experience is an opening to playing better and a bridge to a good time while you're doing it.

This is truly about how any leader of a corporation or captain of a team sets an example, behaving in a way that brings about more positivity, productivity, and most of all, enjoyment. In this case, the leader can be the more seasoned player or anyone who is reading this book.

Side note: Being a seasoned player has nothing to do with age and everything to do with how much one has played and practiced. A twelve-year-old who grew up playing golf will be much more seasoned than a twenty-five-year-old beginner.

An enhanced experience means you are cognizant of your surroundings and playing compatriots, and know how to morph any situation into a positive one. It is appreciated by all parties, even if they don't realize it at the time.

Here are ten ways to enhance your golf round:

1. ***Have a vision of what a successful round looks like.*** Have an intention, be brave enough to claim it, and go after it with gusto. Hold that image in your brain, even if you shank your first tee shot.

2. ***Build a strong belief and stay optimistic about your swing.*** This creates a sense of calm in any circumstance where there is pressure to zone in and hit not just any shot but a true golf shot.

3. ***Have heart, care about others, and don't be afraid to show it.*** Take an interest in your partner or friend's game. You are out there battling the same course and conditions. Take the time to help them find their wayward tee shot(s).

4. ***A great leader or player values and encourages feedback.*** Always being the consummate student, you never know where new knowledge will stem from. Ben Hogan said it best: "I never played a round where I didn't learn something new about the game."[2]

5. ***Appreciate the fact that you've put the time in to improve your game, while respecting and appreciating a fellow player who's still climbing the ladder a few rungs beneath you.*** Remember, you were once them not too long ago.

6. ***Give credit where credit is due.*** Give a positive shout-out or compliment when your playing partners hit a good shot. Positive reinforcement can never be underestimated.

7. ***Your impact reaches beyond your personal performance.*** Exemplify the best of who you are on and off the course. In other words, don't be an a-hole. No gloating, talking excessively, or walking in someone's line.

8. ***Roll with the punches.*** Be able to assess a situation and adjust your style, attitude, and approach to suit the circumstance.

9. ***Feel free to share stories of your struggle with the game or what you are currently working on.*** Just because you can shoot a lower score doesn't mean you're not continually trying to improve your own game. Humility goes a long way.

10. ***While you're at it, share your beer, sandwich, or snacks you have packed.***

    Bonus: Always have a funny story or joke in your back pocket. Lightening the mood is always welcome, no matter where you are or who you are with.

If you can remember two or three of these the next time you loop, then you are well on your way to having an enhanced golfing experience.

ELEVATION EXPANSION

Your comfort zone: The happy place where you can just *be* and relax. That same yet different vibe where you're right at home, living on cruise control and flying on autopilot. Life is good, everything is easy breezy. Familiarity is a warm blanket.

But remember, just as space and time constantly expand, so do *you*. Change is ever present in every moment, every day, whether you realize it or not.

Think about it: 330 billion cells get replaced in your body daily. What seems like solid matter to the naked eye is really millions of molecules in constant motion at a microscopic level. Protons and electrons are infinitely circling nuclei. The water in your shower turns to steam. The ice cube in your drink liquifies. The seasons change on cue every year. The world population shifts daily as 385,000 babies are born every twenty-four hours, while 120 people die each minute. There is no stopping life's constantly changing tides. Like waves in the ocean, you are continually in motion.

You get the point as you expand on the planet at this very moment.

Intentionally moving out of your safe haven is trusting the unknown. It's a leap of faith. When you are in a state of improvement, like studying for an exam, training for a marathon, or working on your golf game, you are consciously directing your life to stretch beyond your comfort level. You are fearless, exploring and embracing the unfamiliar, learning something different, doing the unexpected, and becoming unrecognizable to the person you were a year, a month, or even a day ago.

In conquering the challenge, we are forced to adapt. What was once difficult suddenly feels easy. The choice to do what is beyond the safe and familiar helps us become more adept at facing the *un*safe and *un*familiar.

The only thing within your control that is holding you back from expansion is rooted in the fear of failure. That is, you're anxious about how you will look. Fear holds the lowest vibration. It makes your energy less magnetic and keeps you from things you really deserve. Fear contracts. It blocks any positivity from entering your mind.

In *Power Golf*, Ben Hogan says:

"Fear will influence your muscular reactions, so dismiss all ideas and fears of shooting over water off the tee at a green with water around it, or any other hazards. It is foolish to be frightened by hazards because most players have the club range to miss those hazards if they just swing freely."[3]

Golf is a challenge for any level player. The intention to improve is to choose *courage*. Never be intimidated by missing a shot or losing a match. We never fail, we only learn. Take it easy on yourself, especially if you are new to the game. Understand that to hit a golf shot is to embrace failure and success simultaneously. To miss—and you *will* miss—yet feel brave enough to make a swing again embodies the ultimate character of a human being: to imagine something beyond what you already know, above what you've ever been able to do, and aim to make it a reality.

To be great is not only about winning, it is about the resolve to exceed your own expectations. Having the unwavering determination to improve your game is to venture outside the limits of where you feel at ease and comfortable. Difficult things are good for you. Meet challenges head-on and come to realize that true fulfillment is in overcoming.

It doesn't get easier. You get stronger.

To be great is not only about winning but also about the resolve to exceed your own expectations.

NO MAN IS AN ISLAND UNTIL HE PLAYS GOLF

It is just you and a white ball sitting there, still, quiet, motionless. Waiting to be smacked hard down that fairway. You are alone on your private island with your thumping heart and inner voice, with a stick as your weapon and a ball as your ammo. It simply comes down to what you can generate with the swing you have.

Unlike baseball, the power that you hit the golf ball with is solely based on your own strength, along with the leverage you trigger with centrifugal force. You do not have the benefit of the ninety-mph fastball coming at you to generate power and ball speed. No one is blocking for you like in football. In tennis, you can return a ball well using your opponent's powerful serve to your advantage. The best returners of serves are masters. Andre

Agassi was perhaps the best I've ever seen at the return, turning his opponent's one hundred and twenty-five miles per hour serve against him with passing shots down the line.

When playing golf, the ball is in a resting state, staring blankly at you, daring you to hit it at the target. No one is out there to help you. There is nothing to react to. Just you, a blade, and a ball. It is your responsibility to power that round piece of rubber and thermoplastic resin to the desired location. Perhaps this is why golf may be the most embarrassing sport to play. Every shank or sliced ball into the woods is there for all to see—playing partners and standers-by all have front-row seats to your pain. No one to blame but you. No avoiding accountability. We've all been there, so it's easy to relate. And it always hurts when it happens. No player is immune from these moments.

Golf is not a team sport—it is as individual as it gets. Of course, in the Ryder Cup or Presidents Cup (or LIV Golf) there is a team format, but the reality is each of those guys has to hit their own shots. They are still their own island—their teammates cannot help them hit that pressure tee shot or tricky chip. Each man is responsible for his own shot. In life and in golf, we are given shots to take. How well they go is up to you and your preparation, visualization, attitude, and confidence.

The golf swing itself is such a long, complex, athletic motion. It takes time in the dirt to practice and hone one for yourself. It is much like a sword from medieval times—you must pull it out of the burning fire, pound it and shape it until it's the blade you know you can kill with. In this case, it is your practice time. The swing is an ever-evolving motion, constantly shifting and

morphing as you improve or even as you advance in age.

What is more beautiful than a game that evolves along with you as you move along in life? Personal growth never ends. Your life, like your golf game, is a large oak tree continually and eternally growing toward the sun.

You come into this life alone, and you leave this life alone. When you stand over your slippery seven-footer for par, you are as alone as you'll ever be. No one can make that putt for you but you. It truly is a test of mettle to execute a golf shot under pressure.

To thrive alone under pressure is the ultimate test of personal strength. The game of golf gives you this opportunity each and every time you play...*and* practice, for that matter. Use this space to not only better your golf game but to better yourself. As stated earlier, golf is a metaphor for life. Thrive in life, thrive playing your game, and vice versa.

This beautiful game gives us the opportunity to become better each and every time we play or practice. When we wake up in the morning, we have a chance to be better humans than we were the day before. If you are lucky enough to be awake, then you can appreciate the little things in life. If you get to play a beautiful round of golf in serene surroundings with close friends or family, consider yourself blessed and luckier than most.

Your playing partners may not be able to hit shots for you—that will always be your sole (or soul) responsibility. But when the round is over, you can join them for a drink or a meal, and proudly enjoy the bliss that comes with finishing eighteen and relishing in those few pure shots you hit. Practice paid off, and you have yourself to thank.

THE TAKEAWAY

THE APPLICATION OF MINDFULNESS WHILE PLAYING GOLF IS TO FALL IN LOVE WITH THE PROCESS. It is one of the highest pleasures to be fully immersed in the activity of being present while practicing. It is a childlike, conscious state. And paradoxically, as you take your mind off playing golf, you play better golf.

Practicing in creative ways with structure and efficiency is guaranteed to make you better. Put forethought into your training, understand the aspect of the game you are focusing on, and execute.

Most amateur golfers lack discipline when they train. And as someone who doesn't play on tour, you can spend only so many hours on your game. If your intention is to play better, make the most of your time.

Purposeful practice makes perfect:

- ***Hypnotize yourself:*** Get out of your own way. Play for something. Get used to competition.
- ***Play at home:*** You can work on mechanics from anywhere. Your twenty-minute chip sesh in your backyard pays off more than banging out fifty drivers at the range.
- ***Use technology:*** Shot-track and understand your game better. Know your distances and dive deeper into what skills you need to improve.

- ***Hit your wedges:*** Comfort with your wedges will help boost your confidence within one hundred yards.
- ***Manage the course:*** Ignore the flag and aim for the middle of the green. Prioritize greens in regulation for a lower score.
- ***You will miss:*** Accept where the ball goes and plan for the misses. Knowing this will help you when it happens.
- ***Be tranquilo:*** Your inner calm will help you focus. It will also intimidate your opponents.
- ***Compound interest:*** Consistent progress is a mighty force. Persistence will guarantee improvement. George Washington used to say, "Many mickles make a muckle."[4] That is, the little things add up.
- ***Feel and be:*** How you feel is the secret ingredient to how you will play. Be aware of your mood and get yourself into a positive mindset. Visualize like you are on the course. Take deep breaths and use positive self-talk.
- ***Teach someone else:*** Share this book with friends and fellow playing partners. Be a conduit of information. In teaching others, you continually learn.

This book is like having a golf buddy—keep it in your golf bag as a constant companion to remind you of the simple tools you can use at this moment from anywhere. Give the future you as many opportunities as possible.

When you enact the powers of the mind with intent in the form of visualization and purposeful practice, you will become an unstoppable force to not only become an improved player but a better human being. Use golf as the vehicle you ride to become the best version of yourself.

Break through barriers. Believe in yourself. Trust the process. Exceed your own expectations. Let go of your comfort zone and let golf allow you to move beyond what you think is possible.

Now stand up, stretch your body, and smile. Close the book and go hit some golf balls.

"The greatest pleasure is obtained by improving."[5]

—Ben Hogan

NOTES

ONE

1. Ben Hogan and Herbert Warren Wind, *Ben Hogan's Five Lessons: The Modern Fundamentals of Golf* (New York: Touchstone, 1985), 22.

FOUR

1. "Muhammad Ali Quotes," QuoteFancy.com, accessed September 22, 2023, https://quotefancy.com/quote/869845/Muhammad-Ali-I-am-the-greatest-I-said-that-even-before-I-knew-I-was-Don-t-tell-me-I-can-t.
2. Tom Watson, *Getting Back to Basics* (New York: Pocket Books, 1993), 37.
3. "6 of the Best Miguel Angel Jimenez Quotes," Golf Monthly, July 30, 2018, https://www.golfmonthly.com/features/the-game/6-best-miguel-angel-jimenez-quotes-157022.

FIVE

1. Bruce Lee, *Bruce Lee Striking Thoughts: Bruce Lee's Wisdom for Daily Living* (Clarendon, Vermont: Tuttle Publishing, 2015), 186.
2. Harvey Penick and Bud Shrake, *Harvey Penick's Little Red Book* (New York: Simon & Schuster, 1992), 99.

SIX

1. Jim Lagopoulos et al., "Increased Theta and Alpha EEG Activity during Nondirective Meditation," *The Journal of Alternative and Complementary Medicine* 15, no. 11 (November 2009): 1187, https://doi.org/10.1089/acm.2009.0113..
2. "Alan Watts Quotes," AZQuotes.com, accessed September 22, 2023, https://www.azquotes.com/quote/367869.
3. Neville Goddard, *Five Lessons* (London: Merchant Books, 2012), 107.
1. Neville Goddard, *At Your Command* (New York: Snellgrove Publications, 1939), 17–18.

SEVEN

2. Neville Goddard, *Prayer: The Art of Believing* (London: Merchant Books, 2012), 17.
3. Mathieu Andrieux and Luc Proteau, "Observational Learning: Tell Beginners What They Are about to Watch and They Will Learn Better," *Frontiers in Psychology*, no. 7 (January 29, 2016), https://doi.org/10.3389/fpsyg.2016.00051.

EIGHT

1. A. Vaish, T. Grossmann, and A. Woodward, "Not All Emotions Are Created Equal: The Negativity Bias in Social-Emotional Development," *Psychological Bulletin,* 134, no. 3 (2008), 383–403, https://doi.org/10.1037/0033-2909.134.3.383..
2. "Ben Hogan Quotes," QuoteFancy.com, accessed September 22, 2023, https://quotefancy.com/quote/1241316/Ben-Hogan-I-never-played-a-round-when-I-didn-t-learn-something-new-about-the-game.
3. Ben Hogan, *Power Golf* (New York: Gallery Books, 2010), 178.
4. Boston 1775, "Washington's Mickles in a Pickle," Boston1775.blogspot.com, June 5, 2016, https://boston1775.blogspot.com/2016/06/washingtons-mickles-in-pickle.html..
5. Ben Hogan and Herbert Warren Wind, *Ben Hogan's Five Lessons: The Modern Fundamentals of Golf* (New York: Touchstone, 1985), 16.

ABOUT THE AUTHOR

JOHN ROTA is a Sports Emmy Award winning producer, advertising creative, and business leader whose work spans the media landscape. Passionate about storytelling and developing compelling content, he has crafted programming for top global brands, earning accolades across industries. He believes in the power of purpose and intentional living. He is an avid golfer and is always looking for ways to improve his craft.

THEJOHNROTA.COM